Addiction,

Gravity,

Love

David Atherton

Undeviating, LLC
Reno, Nevada

ISBN: 978-1-7346324-7-7
undeviatingpaths.com

Printed in the United States of America or Canada

Dedication

This book is dedicated to my father, Patrick, my wife, Brandie, and every addict in recovery.

Acknowledgments

Patrick, thank you for getting me to the right re-hab and having the willingness to let me go if I did not complete the program. You're the strongest man I know.

Brandie, thank you for being my favorite addict of all time, my best friend, and showing me how love was intended to be given and received.

Every addict in recovery was on my mind as I wrote this book. No matter how horrific your story is, it can and will get better with effort. Please know that I believe in you and want nothing but the best for you. You matter!

Contents

Addiction, Gravity, Love

Introduction

The moment I admitted I might have a drug problem came when my heroin guy said, "Dave, once I hit this, if I nod off and turn blue, just shove an ice cube in my asshole."

As I attempted to contain the look of disbelief, all I could say in response was, "Oh! No shit, huh?" I played it off like I was all right with this situation, but I wasn't. I was not excited about this scenario whatsoever. I thought at the time: *You mean I have to stick an ice cube into another man's hairy ass so he doesn't die? What the fuck? I didn't sign up for this shit. I didn't get a memo about this situation. There was no rule book given to me.*

What was crazy about the situation was I would've done it. Why not? Get it done! I couldn't let this guy die. I would have to find a new dealer. Not to mention, I might have gone to jail if I'd been found with a dead body. I know I would've absolutely, hands down without a doubt, stuck that ice cube into his butthole. That would have been easy in comparison to some of the other things I did while on drugs.

For me, drugs were the most beautiful explosion

of love and hate. I loved drugs. I loved being high. But they turned on me. The stars in my eyes became bullets of hate and rage. The joy and adventure of drugs became a sick, twisted nightmare. Drugs led to addiction. That addiction led to a gravitational pull that brought me back down to Earth so hard that it broke every emotion in my body, leaving me with no choice but to let love heal me or die.

My philosophy on addiction is this: every single moment of every single day matters. No offense to the "one day at a time" philosophy. I absolutely admire and respect the Twelve Step/Alcoholics Anonymous program. In my sobriety, I've discovered that just getting through today wasn't good enough for me. One day is a long-ass time in the mind of an addict.

By narrowing down each moment, focusing on it, I'm working on present-time thinking. When we focus our attention on each given moment, we find a greater outcome. Let's use making toast as an example. How many times have you made toast while thinking about work, relationships, and responsibilities? I've burnt myself while cooking many times because I was deep in other thoughts rather than focusing on present-time thinking. As an addict, allowing my thoughts to wonder off too far can lead to relapse. Focusing my attention on present-time thinking is crucial for my sobriety. This is where every single moment of every single day matters.

Practicing present-time thinking is a process. If you trust and believe in the process, you will be successful. By trusting the process, you're showing a belief in yourself and the objective you're trying to achieve. When you practice present-time thinking and trust in the process you avoid the feeling of urgency. What I mean by that is you don't feel that weight on your shoulders. You no longer feel the stress, pressure, or urgency to live life in a way that's unhealthy. No need to rush a thing, when you already know you're going to win.

Throughout this book, I will delve into some key concepts that I believe to be the most important concepts of sobriety. I talk about perspective, passion, values, searching, choices, rehab, confronting your addiction, love, and other issues. Each issue represents a concept that I find fascinating in sobriety. These concepts will show how I feel, and I hope they inspire you to create your own helpful point of view.

Take the word perspective: it's your point of view. How you choose to view things dictates how things will be. If you view things as shitty, then shitty you will receive. If you choose to see things as positive, then positivity is what you'll receive.

My point in these concepts is to show you what I developed in my years after rehab. I needed to think of ways to deal with my addiction for years to come. So, like an addict, I overthought everything. I went crazy thinking of the healthiest ways to use my addiction to my advantage. I love that I'm an addict in recovery.

On my journey to discovering these concepts, I remembered key moments in my life. At times, key phrases made an impact on me. One was: "One day it'll all make sense!" I've always loved that line. In life, we are faced with non-stop challenges, and how we handle those challenges dictates our future. "One day it'll all make sense" gave me hope in my decision-making. No matter what I do, at some point this will all make sense. Even when I was an addict and logical thinking was mostly absent, I still believed there was more for me; that one day it would all come together. Sometimes I could only hope that this would all make sense though. As addicts we go through some nasty times.

Throughout my addiction, I shat my pants, threw up at random times, and felt the full effects of withdrawal symptoms' disturbing power. I attempted getting clean on my own at least 40 times. Those failed attempts at sobriety were necessary. I needed to fail. In fact, I needed to fail time and time again. I swore I could do it on my own. Drugs gave me the power to believe I needed no one. I only needed my drugs.

I was truly possessed by my addiction's powers. I have some funny stories about serious shit. I can't believe some of those things happened to me. So, on one hand I laugh, but on the other hand, I almost died. That was the most serious situation I've ever been in.

I use humor to help cope, but also understand the severity of the situation. All of us experience horrific emotional challenges in life. That is in fact a part of life; making fun of some of the shit that happened, helps. Have you ever had to fart, but you held it because you were in front of others? Then you're holding it, and you make a sudden movement, and that fart comes out? It's embarrassing right? Well, I'd squirt shit on myself when I was trying on my own to kick drugs. The withdrawal symptoms make your body jolt so bad that you squirt. It's unavoidable. What I think is funny, is that I've shit myself more as a grown adult than I did as a kid.

I now love life, I love my family and friends, and most of all I love myself. It was addiction that granted me with this opportunity. Addiction was that ugly honesty. Like anything else in this world, the more bullshit you go through, the stronger you get.

In this book I stress optimism. But I had to go through addiction to get to this optimism. While I was addicted, I thought of suicide. I thought of faking my own death and running into the mountains. I had thought after thought about how to escape this situation, and the addiction won every time. All these emotions would hit me like a ton of bricks. I specifically remember these emotions and wrote them out. Here's an example of that initial rehab rage:

I fucking hate life.
I hate my family and friends, and most of all I hate my fucking self.

Everything in this world is ugly, destructive, and filled with greed.

I'm addicted to drugs and see no hope for my future.

I fear sobriety and question the success rate I'm told about in rehab.

I'm ugly, I'm destroying my life, and everything I value means nothing more than an opportunity to manipulate others to attain my drugs.

I'm a fucking mess.

Death is near.

I feel my internal organs shutting down. They ache, they feel weak, and move slow.

My heart beats like a fish out of water gasping for air.

Death is near…
and at this point I welcome it.

I don't want to die but why should I care about my life when this world is filled with destructive greedy ways.

Politics? Religion? I see no love. I see more hate than love.

Religion is supposed to bring me closer to a greater outlook, but I witness so called religious people doing nothing but judging others. Fuck that!

Politics seem to be filled with greed and blatant lies.

Politicians have no love for their countrymen. They only care about their perceived power.

I remember when I felt love every day.

Introduction

I remember when I loved life every day.
I remember loving myself every day.
Addiction took all of that from me.
Death is near.
I feel your presence.
Why won't you fucking take me?
Let's do this. Let's get it over with.
Take me you coward.
Fuck! Why won't I die?
Why won't I just fucking, die?

Throughout the rehab process you address these emotions above. It's the same thing for the addicts who are in recovery but did not go to a rehab. What, how, why, when, where? These are the questions you ask yourself about how you came to this point in your life. I believe the greatest thing you can do in recovery is answer these questions. Understand these questions and why you became addicted.

I look at addiction like my greatest opponent. That voice in my head that's trying to convince me to use is the greatest manipulator I've ever met. I've known this little voice my entire life, and he's good at what he does. He's the slickest, sharpest, smoothest talker I've ever known. I was always confused as to why in one instance, addiction helped me achieve happiness. Then in the next, by listening to addiction's seductive words, I almost died. That voice was a friend, and a foe. Addiction was both helpful and hurtful.

Addiction's ability to convince was impeccable. Like just the tip. Just the tip is just an excuse to stick it all in. We all know this. Just one beer. Just one pill. This consistent convincing that we won't go too far is bullshit. We allow it.

I hear addiction's sneaky whispers every day, but as the years pass, that voice becomes more distant. Envision a man in prison, trying to get the guard's attention. Hands clinched to the jail cell bars, his face pressed in between two of the bars in hope that you will hear him more clearly. His hair crazy, teeth rotten, his entire body is filthy from not showering. He screams for you over, and over again. At times he says sweet things to you, other times he's hurtful. All he wants is for you to give him his fucking drugs. That was the imagery I would see in my mind and hear in my thoughts when getting sober. It took years of practice to get to a point where I embraced him as family. He will forever be in my head, there's no avoiding that, I accept his presence. With that being said, rehab is an opportunity for you to come up with an airtight game plan that beats your opponent down consistently. This opponent will never give up though. He will play dead and wait for complacency. That complacency equals a relapse. That relapse can equal your demise.

This journey back to a life without drugs is such an ugly honesty. It's like this forbidden truth that was hidden from you, and for you to find the truth you must experience the ugly. When you sober up, and truly confront your core issues, you realize how fucked up the world is, but how beautiful your life can be if you make the effort. You spent so much energy trying to cope with society. Trying to fit in, trying to impress others, and trying to claim happiness, were all just a sham that lead you to use drugs to cope. Well, the sham is up. You're awake now. You're getting sober and discovering the real you.

That's the key to all of this—you!

Trying to fit in, and compare yourself to others? Those are self-destructive behaviors. You're an addict. You're naturally different. Trying to impress others becomes demeaning to your true character. My friendship list dissipated immensely when I sobered up.

Trying to claim happiness? It is your responsibility to find happiness every day, and that comes from within you. Happiness is earned by you making an effort every day. No one—and I mean this—no one is responsible to make you happy. When you take your sobriety seriously, earning happiness is extremely attainable. Ugly honesty is the realization that you had things wrong. I had happiness pegged wrong. I'm awake now and recognize how much shit in this world is in my control.

In your past, present, and future, how do you view your sobriety? Sobriety is not only my greatest accomplishment, but it's my way of life. Getting addicted to drugs was the single greatest thing to ever happen to me. I now know the real me and I love what I see. Drugs and alcohol were my best friends. They were great! Drugs gave me confidence. Alcohol gave me courage. Both never let me down. They cared about me when no one else did. They never judged me. They never back-talked me. They were consistent. I knew where I stood with them. I loved what drugs and alcohol once provided. They were my consistent daily fix of happiness. Then they got dark. Then they became destructive. That destruction forced the ultimate question: life or death?

By going to rehab, I chose life. What I perceived as ugly was sheer beauty. What I thought were flaws were precious fortunes. My addictive personality is my greatest gift when that energy is channeled correctly. My willingness to hurt others now became my selflessness to help others. My years of sobriety have been my most beautiful years. As addicts we will go to the greatest—sometimes disgusting—lengths to feed the beast. Why can't I have that same drive for a life of sobriety? I spent so much energy manipulating others to feed my addiction. I now need to spend that same energy manipulating myself into better decision-making. Manipulating isn't always a bad thing. I call it positive manipulating. My wife calls it a healthy form of hustling. It's just finding a different way to get better and be better at being the best you!

All of us as human beings get caught up in society's ways. We all get sucked into the world of materialism, consumerism, selfishness, and greed. We all get sucked into the fears of life—the do's, the don'ts, and social pressure. We are, in fact, all human. We all have hate and evil within us. We all have love and good within us. I am no better than any of you. I am merely a small statistic that happens to look at my addiction as my greatest asset, and my greatest achievement. I believe addicts are the future. All of the most financially successful people in the world have addictive-like behaviors. All of the greatest musicians, athletes, business minds, all have addictive-like behaviors. As addicts, our drive and determination to achieve a goal is different from the average. Just think about the lengths you went to get your drugs. That drive is still within you. That drive is a part of you. You physically went above and beyond to achieve a goal. Yes, it was for drugs. It was for instant gratification. But the point is, you did it. Therefore, you can do it again for the greater good of your future. Find it, and channel it, for the greater good of your sobriety. Drugs give you an instant gratification that destroys your spirit. Sobriety, and practicing a healthy mind, body, and soul, gives you a sustainable lifestyle that allows you to achieve your wildest dreams.

I have worked with mentally ill youth in residential treatment facilities since 2001. In those years I had the privilege to help guide those youth to find a better, healthier way of living. With the proper medication, healthy social skills, and proper coping skills, these young people were able to succeed. While I was in rehab, I thought a lot about those kids. I thought a lot about how I lost sight of my coping skills. With the proper help, I might be able to find them again. I didn't just find my coping skills again, I enhanced them. I worked with hundreds of kids with ADHD. I watched all those hundreds find a way to channel that energy in a healthy manner. Those kids helped me remember that if I see this situation as a gift, then it will be just that.

How do we learn to channel that energy in our years of sobriety? It starts by a reboot. As addicts we need to restart our way of thinking. It starts within each of us. Addicts are forced into this reboot, this restart, when they go to rehab, or find a reason to quit. I've heard numerous stories of women who have gotten pregnant and immediately stopped using. Pregnancy was their reboot. We find no other option. We either change our way of thinking, or we continue the same behaviors. Those behaviors always end with prison or death. By choosing to go to rehab, you take your biggest leap of faith.

One of my main objectives in this book is to encourage you to face that demon every day. Your objective is to be at peace with the things you can and can't control. You've got one life to live and you've already died. Sobriety is a new life filled with a new perspective and new possibilities. Your past is a beautiful history lesson filled with educational information that you will be tested on. Your present is the big exam that you studied so hard for your entire life. Your future is a representation of the information you retained and utilized to your advantage for a life of happiness. You will get some test questions wrong. Go back and get the right answer. Your future depends on it.

I want to stress throughout this book that it is the professionals that helped me through this life or death situation. They helped me through the roughest part. I now have created my own way of living and dealing with my addictive personality.

This book presents a method of finding the real you, loving the real you, and having the drive to achieve things you never thought you could. You went above and beyond to get your drugs, now go above and beyond to get your happiness. You can, you will, you matter. This will get better. It takes time, effort, and consistency. All the years of drugs and alcohol providing confidence, courage, joy, and happiness were nothing more than false hope. False emotions. I once felt like I could conquer the world because of my intoxicated euphoria. This book is me finding that same emotion, sober. "One day it'll all make sense," now makes absolute sense.

So, the question now is, how do you choose to face your addiction? Addiction is suffocating. There's no way around it. The first couple of chapters will address the overwhelming, suffocating truth to it all. But, if you stay with me for the chapters to come, I will show you a different way to approach this ugly situation. In the end, I hope to spark your creative thoughts on how to accomplish your own journey to sobriety. I want you to create your own ways that will inspire you to remain sober.

I understand that relapse is a part of the journey for a lot of addicts. I hope to inspire people to get it right the first time. Bypass the risk. I just hate hearing about those who relapse and die. I am fully convinced that if I use again, I will in fact die. I now choose life. I am not a doctor. I am not a psychologist. I am not a certified professional in drug dependency. I don't have a degree. I have my balls. And you know what? My balls/courage is what kept me alive. The courage to give rehab a try. The courage to confront myself and my issues. The courage to recognize that my addiction is a gift not a curse. I'm not trying to sell you on my way being the end-all be-all. I'm just trying to spark thoughts and ideas within you, to create your own way of dealing with your addiction. Don't forget that you are giving sobriety a chance. That is the most courageous decision you've ever made. Give yourself credit for that.

Addiction is like going into the belly of the beast. You're in it. The question is, will you live? Gravity is the knowledge you obtain when you're in the belly. Searching and discovering the deepest, darkest, aspects to your true self. Love is you getting out of the belly. Finding your way through the fight of all fights. Going through your greatest adversity brought you to your greatest love, you! When you embrace addiction as your biggest challenge, and you pass the test, you learn to love yourself.

Introduction

One of the key philosophies in this book is about finding your personal success. Think about this. I've searched for the reasons certain people are successful. I've questioned the very definition of what is usually termed a success. I've analyzed what drives people to be successful. My favorite common denominator is that successful people are willing to do the things no one else is willing to do.

Ask an addict what they were willing to do to get their drugs every day. Addicts are just as obsessed with success as the highest achievers in the world. Addicts just happened to be going in the opposite direction. But the point is, addicts can achieve success at its highest levels. They just need to channel that success in the right direction.

My belief is that after the opioid epidemic dies down, the survivors will become successful people. After a forest fire, the survivors plant seeds to help rebuild the forest. And that's the thinking behind this book. Addiction is the flame that started the fire. Gravity is the reality and recognition of damage done to the forest. Love is the seeds we need to help rebuild.

ADDICTION: Our lives are filled with learning. We live, we learn. We seek, we conquer. When we conquer, at times, we become addicted to the feeling of achievement. We want what we want, when we want it. Our society is filled with instant gratification. Addiction is a part of all of us. Some control it better than others. Some don't. You could argue that the most successful people in the world are addicted to work. They are driven to accomplish their goal. When that addiction destroys not just an aspect of your life, but your whole life, that's addiction.

GRAVITY: This is Nature's way of bringing you back to reality. Whether you live or die, gravity will bring you back down to Earth from your high. Either way, gravity is that force that keeps you in check. If you fight it, you will lose.

In the world of drugs, gravity is ugly. I remember countless times driving to my dealer's house and trying to convince myself not to go. I didn't want to go because I wanted this addiction to stop. But I just kept driving and went to my dealer's house, every single time. It's as if gravity was pulling me to that house. Addiction made me feel a sense of gravity being horizontal. Gravity can be your rise, or your demise. The choice is yours.

LOVE: In the end, love was my greatest accomplishment. It's pure, it's real, it's within all of us. We all yearn for love. In fact, we want it so badly that we become addicted to searching for it. That addiction creates failure. That failure forces gravity. Gravity forces a foundation of purity. That purity reminds you of the simplicity of life and what it is you want the most. Love!

I hope that after sober people read this book, they will have a better understanding of the addictive mind; the reason behind why addicts do what they do. I believe those who don't have addiction issues will find this book relatable. My belief is that all of us have addictive tendencies, some worse than others. Way worse. But in the end, we are all human, and capable of living a life of happiness and purpose.

I really want to stress that I am no angel. I am still learning every day. I practice these concepts every day. And I am consistently working toward a better life every day. I still struggle at times with anxiety, depression, and anger. I'm just better equipped now at efficiently dealing with those emotions. If there was one thing that I do have, is an unrelenting attitude toward recovery. I want to stress that everything I say in this book is a suggestion. I hope you enjoy.

For the addicts who read this book, this is for you! With this book, I hope to show you how to write your own movie script, write your own album, write your greatest concepts, and more importantly, pave your own path.

Chapter One
Addiction

Have you ever tried something and loved it so much that it scared you—sugar, sex, alcohol, drugs, money, fame, success, etc.? When you first feel it, when you first experience it, that emotion is a life-altering experience. That's the moment where some persist, and some resist.

I grew up in Lake Tahoe, Nevada and looked at the world as a playground. I came from a middle class upbringing where my mother was a high school teacher and my father was a businessman. The two of them were different as can be, but at the same time, they were best friends. I always admired that about them. My mother was a straight A student throughout her life. My father was a "work hard if you want something," "just do it, and get it done" type of personality. I always admired how much fun they had together. That was one of my first examples of how two totally different personalities can live so parallel.

My daily life was to go outside and play with the neighborhood kids. If they weren't around, then I'd ride my bike, skateboard, go swimming in the Lake,

climb trees, catch lizards, and a variety of other out-
door activities. I truly enjoyed interacting with others, but I also had no issue with being by myself. As
far back as I can remember, I loved succeeding in
physical activities and being able to have fun in my
own mind. That's what made life fun for me. Any
time something was fun to me, I would obsess over
it. I never wanted that feeling to leave.

After a sports injury in high school, I was given
pain pills. That's when I first met her—that special
high. I knew immediately that I loved this substance
more than any other. At the time, I had no idea of
my addiction tendencies. My mom was quick to
regulate the amount of pain pills I could consume.
I didn't have the opportunity to get out of control.
But the yearning for that feeling was there. It just lay
dormant for years.

Like a lot of kids, I struggled in school. I was one
of those kids who did not get, or understand, the
system called school. I knew early on I needed to
manipulate my way through all of this. There were
rare moments that I did enjoy learning, but for the
most part I was there to play and socialize. This was
embarrassing for my mother, a teacher. School not
only had come easily for her when she went, but she
loved the educational system. So, for her to have a
son who hated the experience of school and struggled to understand the material, was tough for her.
She was always patient with me though, always loving and understanding. My older brother was the

smart type, you know the type, read the shit once, fully understands and comprehends it? My self-esteem was hurt and very damaged due to my struggles in school. I had yet to discover that my method to learn was all right for me, and that as an adult I would not struggle. At the time, I thought, "I'm going to be dead at a young age because my brain isn't wired correctly, and I won't survive long." Sports ended up saving me, providing me self-esteem and giving me joy.

I was a social kid in school. I enjoyed interacting with peers and excelled in the world of recess. As a child, I loved being around others who were happy. I loved seeing the world as a happy place. So, when we had to go back into school after recess, I felt confused. Why did the fun end?

I very much enjoyed being happy, and I wasn't about to let school drag me down into depression. As a kid, I didn't understand true struggle and responsibilities. You just go for happiness every day. It's fascinating how puberty destroys all of that. What the fuck happened? As a little guy every day, I searched and found happiness. Then puberty hit. The two things that made me happy were sleeping, and masturbating.

My upbringing was surrounded by nature: small town, small schools, blended with big nature. It was a beautiful upbringing that later in life I took for granted. Growing up in a small town has its perks and it's down sides. I enjoyed being well known by my peers. I also enjoyed knowing who everyone was. What I didn't like was everyone knowing your business. I've been a private person throughout my life, and I couldn't wait to leave once I graduated high school.

My mother and I were going to the grocery store one day when I hit her with the fact that I had smoked weed for the first time. I was in fifth grade. My mother was shocked, her face turned red, and the sound of silence made my brain feel like it was going to pop. Once my mother gathered her thoughts, the first thing she said was, "Thank you for being honest, David." There was more to the conversation, of course, but the point was that my foundation of honesty had just been set. I knew this moment would help me in my future.

Make the most of each day by any means necessary. When I liked something, I went hard at it. Most kids are crazy about sweets. I was no different. When it came to drugs and alcohol, it was no different than sugar. Once I tried anything that I liked, I really liked it.

I loved the rush of success. When I succeeded in sports I felt an instant bond. I knew in my heart that I would do this for the rest of my life. No matter what happened, I would not allow anything or anyone to stop me from pursuing that activity. That outlook on sports transferred into my daily life. Any time I felt the effects of happiness, or a dopamine rush, I felt it would be a lifelong relationship. Sports, riding bikes, climbing trees, swimming, eating sugar, were all a part of that rush.

My addiction to opiates started in high school when I got my first taste of pain pills after a surgery. Being a football guy, I had my share of injuries and required a couple of different surgeries over the years—and with those procedures came pain pills. The first time I experienced morphine coursing through my veins, I couldn't believe the feeling of peacefulness. I swore I was all right with dying. That joy and euphoria, I knew deep down was going to be a problem. For years, I secretly knew how much I loved that high, but didn't have a deep enough desire to pursue it. At some point, I knew I would re-connect with opiates. It's like an ex-girlfriend who you know you shouldn't mess with again, but the sexual pleasure is worth the agony.

Alcohol was my baby step. All along I knew I yearned for more, but alcohol got the job done for a lot of years. I loved drinking. I loved going out and being social. I loved clubs. I loved casinos. I loved how alcohol inspired me to behave irrationally, then allowed me to blame it for my bad decision-making. Alcohol never got upset with me for using it as an excuse for my mishaps. Alcohol was consistent and easily accessible.

When I was living in Missouri, I got a DUI outside of a fast food joint. It was the end of a party night and I needed some food to top it all off. As the officer's lights flashed on me, I pulled over in the parking lot of this fast food joint, taking up two spots—failing at my first attempt to prove that I was sober.

The officer approached the car and asked for my license. As he checked it, he asked me the normal questions: "Sir, where you headed tonight? Where do you work? Are you a college student? Sir, have you had any alcohol tonight?" He then asked me to step out of the car.

As I was talking to this officer, I couldn't help but think he was a cool individual. Very polite—which inspired me to be polite back. He then asked if I could walk a straight line for him. I said "yes" with pure confidence, sure pacing a straight line would be an easy "A" for me. My sense of balance was my greatest athletic quality. In my mind, asking me to walk a straight line was like asking Michael Jordan to shoot a basketball at the hoop, and make it. This straight line was about to be my bitch.

Before I made my attempt at this line there was a needed pep-talk. I've been nervous in a lot of situations and every situation I gave myself a quick pep-talk. I needed to remind myself of all my athletic achievements. I visualized walking this line with pure confidence. This moment was my opportunity to shine and show this officer that I was not intoxicated.

I took my first step and felt a sudden earthquake under my ankles. I couldn't believe the forces of gravity had a problem with me in that moment. My confidence quickly depleted. My second step was tentative and uncertain. I felt as if I'd suddenly become the most uncoordinated individual on the face of the Earth.

My third step—I fell flat on my face. I was embarrassed, but still somewhat convinced that I was a phenomenal athlete. I got up, dusted off, and made another attempt at it. Only to be met with the same results. I looked like a guy who had just been knocked out by Mike Tyson: legs wobbly, trying to get up and prove to the ref that I'm good to go. Only to get a close look at the pavement again.

After my failed second attempt, I stood up, stuck my chest out, and tried to compose myself with pride. I made eye contact with the officer. That was a bad move. He looked like my mother, disappointed at me. I slouched with my head down admitting defeat without words.

The officer smiled knowingly and asked, "Do you think I need to put you in handcuffs, or are you all right?"

I said, "No, you don't have to do that. Can I ride up front with you, though?"

"Sure Mr. Atherton." Off to jail I went with my new friend Officer Cool Guy.

When I was bailed out the next day, the first thing I did was go out and buy some beer. My license was revoked for 30 days, so I stayed home and got drunk for a month.

My addiction to alcohol was filled with an acceptance of depression. Alcohol made me feel good. In fact, it made me feel great. It numbed the reality I was desperately trying to avoid. That's the greatest aspect to drugs and alcohol. I did not understand how to live in this world any longer. I felt that reality just wasn't for me.

I wanted to be liked by my peers—in fact, I wanted to be liked by everyone. That was, of course, not feasible or realistic. But when I was drunk, I thought I was liked by more people than I could count. I loved to work the room with my infectious personality that was filled with positivity. Alcohol made this possible. Alcohol created the personality I always wanted to have. Like most addicts, I didn't think that personality was possible while sober.

Hangovers were a mild form of withdrawal symptoms for me. There's nothing mild about them for a serious alcoholic. For me, they were a warning that I ignored. Depression was a regular emotion with these hangovers. I ignored the depression as well. I felt like being drunk was my small window of happiness. Slowly, my binge drinking morphed into a nightly thing. On days off, it was an all-day thing. Wake up, have a beer for breakfast.

Alcohol gave me the freedom to live carefree—at least at night. By day, I was often guilt-ridden. At night, sex without a condom seemed just fine. The next day, I would be filled with remorse, guilt and fear. The best way to ignore those feelings was to start drinking again. The best way to ignore any form of reality? Start drinking again.

When I was addicted to drugs and alcohol, I would find myself in bittersweet situations. When I got liquor, or smoked heroin—or chased the dragon, as it's called—I would love the fact that I was getting high, but also feel sad because after the bottle or hit I would need to find more. Addiction is a never-ending whirlwind game of seek and destroy. Being high is what it was all about.

Heroin: oh, how sweet it was. Talk about a journey into the unknown. Even though I had heard a thousand times throughout my life to steer clear of it, heroin took me places I never imagined possible.

As a kid, I noticed a reoccurring pattern of celebrities dying from drug overdoses. John Belushi, River Phoenix, and Chris Farley are some examples. Even before that, I remember my Dad speaking of Jimi Hendrix, Janis Joplin, and Jim Morrison. These were all extremely talented individuals. My young mind believed that heroin must be the most magical drug on earth. Those were talented people and I wanted to be talented, too. Being that I loved a challenge, and was willing to take risks, I knew someday I would try heroin.

Heroin was like winning a championship. Athletes talk about winning championships and the emotions that come with it. Professional competitions take hard work, sacrifice, determination, and passion, but it's all worth it when you work so hard for it. Well, getting your drugs every day takes hard work, sacrifice, determination, and passion. You have to devote yourself to this one mission every day. The days that you fail in getting your drugs, that's like losing the big game. When I was an addict, I'd much rather lose any sports championship than ever suffer withdrawal symptoms from heroin.

I hated when my dope was a dud. Black tar heroin was my shit. I loved chasing the dragon. When my dope was weak and cut down, it added to my frustrations. Dealer after dealer, they cut this product down to maximize profitability. They know you'll be back, you're an addict, and you're predictable. If you think about that concept in the drug game, it becomes frustrating to continue buying that product. Oxycontin was consistent. Heroin was a gamble.

When you're addicted, you'll take that chance every time with heroin. That stress is there, though. You fear not getting high because you're not sure what this batch of heroin has to offer. With Oxy or pain pills in general, you know what you're getting. The mission is to get high. Every single day of my addiction, that was the single most important aspect of my day. When it comes to consumerism, you want to maximize your opportunity to achieve that goal. When you're an addict you will take the greatest risks to possibly achieve that goal. Meaning, you'll maximize your opportunity because the risk reward is worth it every time.

Withdrawals keep the addiction going. Withdrawals are like the bully bodyguard that beats your ass for disrespecting addiction. My favorite drug of them all was Oxycontin. I always called it Mr. Consistent—Oxy is consistently the same. Heroin is a gamble, because so many dealers would cut it up. Oxy remained faithful, and loyal, which made Oxy my favorite drug of all time. Heroin was like a dirty girl. I loved her. She was dirty, dark spirited, and freaky, but sometimes she turned on me. One day she was beautiful, the next day ugly as fuck. Oxy was built like a thoroughbred horse: powerfully built, perfect smile, beautiful walk, and always the same.

This type of thinking is addiction. When you're addicted to drugs, your view of daily life is unbelievably skewed. When I was on drugs, I was lying every day. I hated who I was, but I'd act confident, laughing and playing it cool. I covered up how I was truly feeling, masking my fucked-up self.

Withdrawal symptoms—and when I was in rehab, we called them "withdrawals" for short—make you feel the most devastating loss. Withdrawals make you consider suicide—but if you commit suicide, then you won't get to do drugs anymore. You have no choice but to strategize, work even harder than before. You are now zoned in like a top-notch athlete ready for your biggest game.

I now know addiction in its entirety. I traveled and explored the world of drugs. I felt the intoxicating joy that drugs provided, and I loved it. I felt the full effects of addiction's misery— that gravitational pull that takes you places you never should go. And in the end, I lived it. When I faced my addictive demons, I dealt with the biggest challenge to my existence. Mentally, I reclaimed my health. I discovered the power of the mind and still have so much to learn.

Addiction created the saddest, most painful memories I've ever felt. It stripped me of the natural grieving process. Those who I loved and died while I was on drugs; I can't ever have those moments back. Addiction forced a selfish side to me that was pure evil. I even stole pain pills from my ailing mother to feed my addiction. She blamed others for her missing pills. I sat quiet, admitting to only a few. I'll never get to apologize. I'll never get to hug her and say how sorry I am. I can't prove to her that I am a better man now. That I beat addiction. I want to go back in time and love her better for her last couple years. I'll never get to do that.

An addict learns to live with regret. Addiction teaches you to regret shit, then forget shit. The regret stems from being sober. You quickly forget again, once you get high. It tears you apart so bad emotionally, that physically you are drained. Regret is like a rearview mirror that you're forced to look at. Emotionally you feel shame, embarrassment, guilt, and disappointment from these past decisions. All those emotions trigger impulsive decisions, especially when you're under the influence. Any logical decision making you have, fades. When I felt the emotions of shame, I knew deep inside I needed to work on myself. But the more I looked at myself, the less I liked what I saw. I wanted to get back to a life of normalcy, but I felt stuck in the emotions of quick-sand. I needed to climb a mountain to get back to normalcy. All the while, you continue to use. In the world of addiction, the only option out of the misery is by doing more drugs. So, I accepted regret as part of my life every day.

Going to rehab doesn't seem like an option. When you're addicted, you think about rehab because you get sick of the pain. Your addictive thoughts quickly put you back in your place and lead you to using again. Addiction doesn't allow you to believe in hope. There is no hope. You just need to minimize how much you're using per day. Then the next day comes, and you go harder than ever before. This continues over and over. There's no stopping it. There's no hope. No one's going to save you. No one is going to go through withdrawals for you. The sooner you accept that, the better. That was my thought process every day.

I've heard people over the years ask, "Why don't they just stop? They see what they're doing to their family and friends. Why not just stop?" Addicts are dealing with a state of mind that is enduring a force beyond their comprehension. Jump off the roof of your house; feel the forces of gravity. There's no way for you to defy it. It's one of Nature's greatest powers. That's addiction. Every time I fed the addiction, every time I left to go get my dope, I felt addiction's powerful force. It felt no different than jumping from the roof. I can't remember how many times I told myself, "Don't do it man. Don't do this," as I was on my way to get my drugs.

My entire life I thought moderation was the dumbest fucking word. Moderation was like telling a girl "just the tip," then actually doing just the tip. Fuck moderation. Fuck balance. Go balls to the walls. I've always felt that way ever since I was young. My attitude toward moderation came from my success with taking risks. Being willing to take risks equaled happiness. Happiness for me was when I did things at 100 percent. That made the most sense to me. I failed a lot when I was young, but I was proud that I took risks. I felt moderation was a sign of weakness. Having self-discipline, restraint, or self-control felt like I was holding back my true self. Every time I did contain myself and have self-discipline, I felt a bit of frustration. This internal conflict made me dislike the concept of moderation.

Looking back, I always wore different masks to the world, and hid what was really inside me. Drugs made it easier to hide. I put on a show every day to hide who I truly was. Pretending I was a good kid. I didn't want to embarrass my mother and her reputation as a teacher she had earned within the community. Once I got older, I started to accept that I was in fact a good person. I just had a dark side to me that I loved—and that side loved drugs and alcohol. Is that so bad? I often wondered if I was a bad person for embracing that part of myself. Addiction showed me how confused I was, and I felt very alone in that process.

Falling in love with football helped me be addicted to something, and it made me look good. I hid my internal issues and convinced myself it wasn't a problem. Football allowed me to hold back the demons for a while. But at the same time, I had internal emotional issues going on. I wanted to do drugs and alcohol, but at the same time, I wanted to be healthy for football. I wanted to be more outgoing with others, but felt I needed drugs and alcohol to do so. I wanted a girlfriend because society made me feel I was supposed to. Football required my attention, so a girlfriend was out of the question. I'm left-handed and feel like the world wants me to be right-handed. I hated school, but felt like the world was telling me I would never succeed without school. I felt consistent confliction within my thoughts. A part of rehab is addressing your issues as far back as you can remember. Being able to travel back in thought, and remember my behaviors as a child, helped me identify where my addiction-like behaviors originated.

A lot of the issues you need to address are things you regret. I regret not putting more effort in school. I regret not trying harder in baseball. I regret not fighting back when I was put in a head lock by a high school kid. I know those things sound unbelievably small, but they matter. Any moments in life that we look back on and regret can play a role in how we behave currently. If those emotions are not correctly dealt with, then they start to weigh on your psyche and lead to bad decision-making.

Some of the other issues that pop up are things that you don't like about yourself. When you look in the mirror and don't like what you see. It could be your physical appearance, or your emotional state. At times there are things we don't like about our own personalities. Those issues consume us and the best way to ignore those emotions is through addiction.

Looking back and identifying where we failed at dealing with those emotions, is where we learn to address them responsibly now.

I find it interesting to look back and think of all my failed attempts at dealing with my addiction. Who was that guy? Was that really me? I tried stopping my addiction with exercise, healthy eating, and doing more activities in nature. I would watch chick-flicks to help tap into my sensitive side. I would listen to love songs in hope of softening my hard addiction shell. I never once thought I needed to address my view of the world or myself. It's interesting to look back now because it's one more example of me learning things the hard way. As long as I keep learning.

Have you ever watched a scary movie and that one character who always goes toward the danger? The whole town knows there's a mass murderer on the loose. Everyone is frightened. The person in the movie hears a noise in the basement. Instead of calling the police, getting a weapon, getting their car keys and making a dash, they instead walk down the staircase to the basement. Then to add to this, as they're walking down the narrow staircase, floor creaking, the lights cut out. Then this dumbass individual says, "Hello? Is anyone there?"

You as the viewer, you are logical. The individual going down the staircase is illogical. As a logical person you do what makes the most sense. You make responsible decisions. All of us have that logical side to us, but not when you're addicted to drugs. That dumbass in the movie going toward the danger, that's the addicted side of a person. The viewer, disappointed in that dumbass, that's the sober side of a person. That's what happens when you're addicted to drugs. You know you're making dumbass decisions. You know you shouldn't go down that staircase, but you do it anyway.

It's crazy to think about how risk/reward works for an addict. Those hooked on drugs will gladly take the chance of risking death to get high. They will gladly take the chance of going to jail/prison to feed the beast. That's what we deal with in the world of addiction.

Addicts have a drive and determination while under the influence that is bar none. Addicts will go to disgusting, disturbing, unfathomable lengths to get their drugs. If they go to rehab, get the proper treatment, and channel that energy for the right reasons, there's no stopping them from success. If they could take that same energy they had as addicts, and apply it to their life of sobriety, wouldn't they be more likely to succeed? Once again though, channeling that energy correctly is vital.

I've always admired people who channel their determination to be successful. We admire certain people in this world because of their success. We admire their work ethic. We admire their drive and determination to complete a task. We admire the training, the studying, and the obsessing over being the best at what they do. They have a wiliness to do all the things nobody else wanted to do.

Well, I did the same thing every day to get my pills and heroin. I was willing to do all the things no one else was willing to do. I did exactly what I needed to do to achieve my goal. I did not allow anyone to get in my way. I did not allow friends or family to distract me from achieving my goal. My focus, determination, and obsession with achieving this goal was professional.

Why the fuck am I supposed to ignore those behaviors as a sober person? Those behaviors are wonderful traits. If I channel those behaviors for the right reasons, then I'll be not only successful in my sobriety, but also in my future of achieving whatever it is I desire. I have those good traits. I have those good qualities. I used those qualities as an addict, so now I'm going to use them as a sober man.

I failed at getting sober time and time again. I tried kicking 40 plus times. I failed every one of those times. I failed over, and over, and over. I couldn't get clean alone. The truth was, I needed help. I gave rehab a chance. It provided the help I needed, and I was able to get sober.

Failure is necessary when you're in search of success. I needed those moments of failing at kicking. I needed to feel failure. Now I fully understand success, because I failed so good. I'm proud of my addiction and the failure I experienced. It's as if I told myself to go fuck up. Go be the best at fucking up. Go destroy your life. Go make some bad decisions. Go destroy friendships. Go burn some bridges. Go break as many laws as you can without getting caught. Go bareback with as many women as you can. Take as many drugs as you can. Drink as much as you can. Go build that bond with death. Because in the end, you're ridding yourself of the current you. Deep down inside, you know you hate that person in the mirror. You've disliked that person for years. Now it's time to give yourself credit, not criticism. All these bad decisions led you to rock bottom. When that happens and you're ready to start the new you, rehab is where you belong. You have the opportunity to shape yourself, mold yourself, into the person you've always wanted to be. So many people, including sober people, want an opportunity to start anew. Have a clean slate. Welp, you as an addict have been granted that golden opportunity. Take full advantage of it. You fucked up good. You destroyed your life. When it comes to failure, you succeeded.

Does addiction suck? Absolutely. In fact, I think the word "suck" doesn't do it justice. For those of us who live to tell the tale, tell the story of success.

Addiction is the single most powerful, over-whelming, manipulative, destructive force that I have ever felt. It is a beast that feeds off human emotion. Every emotion I had, became a part of the addiction. Surviving that made me rethink everything about life. Addiction is now my greatest asset.

Exercise

In this chapter, the objective is to identify your addictive personality, even if you are sober, or fresh out of rehab. This process takes honesty, so don't bullshit yourself.

How frequently do you see this addictive personality? Identify your addictive side. Write these examples down on a sheet of paper. Type it out. Use a dry eraser board. Doesn't matter what you use, as long as you can see this and read it every day. Identifying where you might show sides of your addictive behaviors is vital.

Once these are written down, read them. Circle the ones you need to address first. So, if you consume too much sugar every day, and you know it, circle that one. How you do that is up to you, but make eliminating these things a non-negotiable situation. Do what's necessary to win.

What helped me was addressing those negative issues and behaviors piece by piece. Some things took no time at all. Some took a lot of effort.

There's no need to rush when you know you're going to win!

Chapter 2

Withdrawals

Withdrawals are the reason I was addicted to drugs. The effects of addiction withdrawal—which we called "withdrawals" in rehab—led me to making unimaginably bad choices and decisions. Withdrawals are like being in a heavyweight bout with someone four times your size, just beating the dog piss out of you. You can't even fight back because you're so weak. You have to take this ass-whooping for a good week unless you tap out—meaning you got ahold of some drugs, and the ref (you) stops the fight.

What makes withdrawals so disturbing is that you're the sole witness to a side of yourself that you never thought you were capable of, and you watch in disbelief. Withdrawals create a desperation within you to do whatever is needed to ease the pain. At times, this desperation can consist of you breaking the law. Stealing is a very common behavior because you need to obtain money. Lying to friends and family on why you need to borrow money is also common. Another desperate attempt to ease the pain is by consumption. I would take mass amounts of ibuprofen thinking it would help. It never did. I would take over-the-counter sleep meds in mass amounts thinking that would help. It never did. I would try to drink beer in hopes that it would help. That didn't work either. At one point, I stripped naked, got in a bathtub, and attempted to drink a cold beer in my butthole in hopes that it would get me drunk faster. It didn't work because the temperature of a cold beer in that warm cozy region made me jump out of the tub like a cat to water. These moments of desperation show a very intense side to your fight or flight response system. What's crazy is that they are both working at the same time. It's not one or the other, it's a matter of which one will help first. Your fight response is trying to consume things in hopes that it works, and your flight response is attempting to leave that situation by solving the riddle of how to get money and obtain the drugs. Trying to describe to people the effects of withdrawals is a challenge. Unless you've lived it, you'll never really grasp it.

Here's sort of what it's like: let's say you're afraid of spiders. Suddenly, one runs out in front of you on the kitchen floor. You panic and feel fear coursing through your body. Maybe you run out of the room. The moment you're away from the spider, you start to feel a level of relief due to creating a distance between you and the spider. When that spider was right there in your face, just the sight of him freaked you out. You stopped breathing. That fear made you panic. But when you ran away from it, you created space between you and the threat. You could start to gather yourself and come up with a plan for that uninvited guest.

When people go through withdrawal from opiates, there is no distance between the panic and the thing you fear. That fear and the panic that you feel throughout your body doesn't leave. When you run from that spider you create an opportunity to gather your thoughts. You don't get to run from withdrawals. Gathering your thoughts and coming up with a plan doesn't happen. Imagine feeling that fear, panic, and anxiety for a solid minute. It's intense! Now imagine feeling that for a full week, with no sleep. That's just a small idea of what it's like to suffer from withdrawal.

Ever have the flu? You have the shits, then you throw up. You have the shits some more, then you throw up some more. The flu is weak in comparison to withdrawals. When I went through withdrawals, the first shit I took would be obscene; just a mammoth in comparison to a normal one. Once that one big shit passed, it was anxiety shits from then on. Anxiety shits are like feeling the cramps of a massive shit, only to sit on the toilet and spew a shot glass full of diarrhea. The cramps are intense: the pain pulsates, and you naturally try to push for more to come out. Nothing but pain comes out. That's another aspect to withdrawals.

Have you ever experienced heartbreak? It's a devastating feeling, and you find yourself making absolutely crazy decisions. You might call the person over and over and cry. You can't eat, can't sleep. It's misery. Your brain tends to fixate on the possibility of fixing the problem. You try to think of something else, but you just can't. Every move you make reminds you of the good times you shared. You try your best to remember the fun memories, but you're abruptly met with the reality that it's all over. After days of this misery, you find yourself wearing dirty clothes, and you smell like rat piss mixed with the smell of your corn-nut infested feet. That's a taste of the mental anxiety you feel during withdrawal.

Have you ever worked out so hard that you were shocked by the amount you sweated? Or when you go to a humid climate and you find yourself outdoors longer than you wanted? Now you're drenched in your own sweat. Withdrawals make you sweat like that. The sweat feels hot to the touch. Your sweat feels like it's cooking your skin. Then within a flash, you're freezing cold. As if you were in Antarctica. You grab blankets to get warm, but then your blankets are wet and nasty with the smell of your toxin-infested sweat. The hot sweats and cold chills fluctuate back and forth.

Have you ever had a leg or muscle cramp? Sometimes, the cramp hits so hard and is so painful that your entire body jolts. In withdrawals, those jolts hit even harder—you'd swear it's going to break a bone. Your muscles constrict with the power of a python. When people say, "kicking drugs," they mean literally kicking. Your legs kick with such fury that you don't know what to do. You don't know how to counteract this situation. Truth is, you're fucked! At times, rocking your body back-and-forth gives you a split second of relief. As if my mother was holding me and trying to rock me to sleep. I'd lie on my side and rock, and that would hold off the jolting and sweating... for maybe a second or two.

There were a couple times during withdrawals that I saw some seriously weird shit. I saw a dark shade above my head floating around like a cloud. I might have been hallucinating—that wouldn't surprise me. It could've been a car driving by at night-time, and the reflection off of the ceiling gave an appearance of a dark shade—but it happened a few times. During these experiences, I felt the presence of something. My body was shutting down and I felt the presence of something near. I can downplay it as me tripping out mentally because of the condition my body was in. Or I can tell you what I believed to be happening: Death was fucking near!

Withdrawals are your body and mind's way of spitting out an unwanted guest. Addiction wants you to make those guests roommates. With that, the only way to stop this torture is by getting your drugs back into your system.

Withdrawals are a horrific experience, and I experienced some nasty ones. I was on a business trip in Detroit, Michigan, when this incident occurred. I was staying at a hotel, it was a Saturday afternoon and I had run out of my pills the night before. I decided to go to the liquor store to get some alcohol in hopes that it would help with my symptoms. As I pulled up to the store, just the sight of the liquor in the store windows made my stomach turn. The warning cramps had started, and I was worried I might be sick. I instantly started sweating fear. I walked in the store looking like shit: my face was red from the anxiety and sweat was dripping down my face. I was wearing a t-shirt that was wet from perspiration. I was also wearing my favorite white cargo shorts. I loved those shorts.

I found the vodka, but suddenly my guts really started hurting, and I knew I had to go—soon! As I approached the counter I could barely walk; I was attempting to control the unavoidable explosion. I must have looked like a zombie as I approached the check-out.

I got to the register expecting the store clerk to ask if I was all right—but he did not. My guess was he'd seen that behavior before. He probably figured I was just another junkie who just happened to be wearing beautiful white shorts. I purchased my vodka and made my way to the car. The cramps were getting worse.

The hotel was only two blocks away, so I hoped that I would make it back in time. On the drive back, I hit two stoplights that happened to be the longest stoplights in the history of America. The closer I got to the hotel, the stronger the cramps got. The sweating continued, and drool flowed down my chin.

I was relieved when I reached the hotel parking lot. But that's when I realized I had another problem: it felt like I had to walk from one end of Texas to the other to get to the safety of my bathroom. I dropped my keycard, and bending over made things that much worse.

I finally got into the building and stared at the never-ending hallway to hell. I couldn't believe how far that room appeared to me. Every step down that hall was a struggle. I was clenching my butt cheeks with every step. Cramps were still kicking the hell out me, and the sweat was still dripping down my body.

Oh no! I thought as shit started draining down my legs and onto the floor. I ran to the room, unlocked the door, and practically threw myself on to the toilet... only to discover I had no more shit left. I had voided myself onto the hallway floor of this very nice hotel.

Although I was mortified and embarrassed, I knew my next move was to quickly clean up. I threw away my favorite white—now brown—shorts. Grabbing a pile of towels, I went out into the hallway stark naked, and, on all fours, scrubbed the shit off the hallway floor. Luckily no one came out of their rooms.

Once I finished, I went back to my room, partly propping the door open while I got some clean clothes and gathered the feces-infested towels and clothing to throw out. Suddenly, I heard voices in the hallway— a family. As they passed, a young boy said, "Ew Momma! What's that smell?" I looked out into the hallway, and had a very brief and uncomfortable moment with the mom—we made eye contact. She had to have seen the panic in my face, the madness in my eyes. She put her hand on her son's shoulder and said, "I don't know, baby. Let's get out of here." After a minute or two, I gathered the courage to walk outside and throw out the dirty laundry into the dumpster.

Stories like this happen to most addicts. I shared stories with a variety of people in rehab and for the first time since my addiction, I felt a connection. It was nice to know I wasn't alone in these disgusting moments. Sharing these experiences with others helped me distance myself from the lie. Confronting the truth, and using humor to do it, helped me cope with my deepest issues. Humor became our new drug, so we all shared some of our craziest stories.

Withdrawal symptoms are disgusting situations that are filled with embarrassing moments. I was encouraged in rehab to express these moments or write them down, then share them with someone. Getting it off your chest is the point. At one point in my path to sobriety, I wrote a poem about my interpretation of withdrawal symptoms.

What you're about to read is a little writing I created to help cope with the emotions of recovery, and what I remember about withdrawals. I call it "My Broken Rhythm."

My experience in the realm of withdrawals was complex. Its effects were consistently crushing and persistently painful. The rainfall came from a storm that was mythical. The typical sensation was pins and needles throughout my entire frame. Nothing sane about this place, the man in the mirror looks dead and fake. My fate has always been to get close to death, but not die. Just try to live life fast and hard. No regard to the weatherman reporting a storm filled with drama. And Momma always said don't talk to strangers, but I ignored that as well. Hell, once opiates hit my system the deal had already been made. He'll get paid, I just didn't know like this. The suicide kiss almost made sense to me. Regret to me, is a pointless thought that's incorrect to me. He's here to collect, everything to fear, no room to correct, death must be near.

The first thing I always felt was the anxiety. A variety of hopeless feelings and hyperventilating through the ceilings. I questioned each breathe, questioning is this death. The stress was like an elephant taking a rest on my chest with his best of friends. As the anxiety increased so did the fecal matter, with that came the splatters, an uncontrollable flush and rush of my bowels making moves through the groves of my sickness.

I'm the witness to this horrific event. Can't repent it's too late, the toxins are in route for the great escape. Contrary to popular belief, this isn't a two-day thing. What I'm facing is a non-stop throwing up and shitting fest. And let's get the next one on deck, the infamous sweats. Don't forget that every toxin in your body is in fight or flight mode. On this road, within seconds I'd be sweating boiling liquid, conflicted now because the sweat changed its face, now what's seeping at a rapid pace is liquid ice. I'm freezing to death in the bed of a beat down hotel room.

I'm forced to consume a non-stop anxiety, the urge to shit, hot and cold sweats won't quit, now I got an uncontrollable twitch that's like an itch I can't scratch. My arm muscles jerk with rapid force, and of course don't forget the legs. They call it kicking a drug for a reason. The darkest season is upon me. Death is near and it's becoming loud and clear. My fucking bones ache with agonizing pain from the insane leg kicks. Bones feel like sticks, muscles constrict, and it feels like the crackling of wood on the brink of a break. My weight feels like 2 tons of flesh on the verge of falling through the floor. The core of the earth pulls me closer to its depths.

These physical effects aren't the only thing, now to the mental aspects of the devil's symphony. Rapid thoughts, same thoughts on repeat, memories of my past just beat like a drum with no rhythm to it. Repetitive song versus race at a pace I can't control. Every minute's like an hour, every hour's like a day. My thoughts say to get that chemical of choice. My voice of reason is dead. It's time to lie, rob, steal, cheat, spit, scratch, claw, beat. Suicide is an option but it's not the go-to. *If I end my life, then how can I continue my drug use? I don't know if there's drugs in the afterlife. No wife, no kids, nothing to show for a life of happiness. Fuck this, I'm over it. It's either death or drugs.*

I choose drugs bitch! I ain't stopping now. This is my choice, and this is my addiction. Maybe it's in confliction with what society thinks I should do, but guess what, fuck you! Fuck the systems, fuck this country, fuck the rich, fuck your money, fuck religion, fuck politics, fuck this life, fuck all this shit. Society is filled with ugly ass hate and I'm to remain sober and think of a better day? You stay sober, I chose dope. I can't stop thinking, I can't stop stressing, I can't stop shitting, I can't stop sweating. My life is miserable, and I know it. Too proud to show it, but the truth is I need help! I need help.

Then the evil voice within says…

Calm down, drama queen. Save your steam for the plane we got to catch. We've only scratched the surface of our purpose you little fuck. Keep it together. Forever we're on a mission to put these symptoms in submission. Keep the vision at the forefront of your mind. Get back on the grind and let's feed this beast. For this feast we need greed, some speed, and just a seed of how we can go get some money. Funny how you're bitching about the symptoms of addiction and the possibility of you and I parting ways. You must be dazed and confused if you think cupids going to save your stupid ass. The deals been made motherfucker now go get us some drugs. Don't forget who I am. Don't forget what I'll do. Don't forget the big plan. Don't forget that I'll fucking end you. Now go get us some fucking drugs.

Every single day I remind myself of this situation; of these emotions. Death was talking to me. He was right there ready to take me. For whatever reason, I lived. I'm here.

I clearly remember the feeling of my internal organs slowly shutting down. What made that feeling so surreal was that I accepted death. I had zero thought of rehab or of living. I was just trying to accept that I was going to die soon and be at peace with it. Withdrawals take so much energy from you that death sounds peaceful. What creates the dilemma is addiction. Your addiction needs drugs. You can't keep feeding the beast drugs if you're dead.

I've met a few elderly people in my life who told me they felt death was near. They could feel their organs slowing down. They felt their body slowing down. They all reported being at peace. I remember that peace. I felt that exact feeling in the weeks leading up to my overdose. When I came out of the coma three days later, I felt a peace of mind that represented clarity. I was content. I obviously had a huge mountain to climb in the world of sobriety, but there was a sense of peace.

I don't believe that death is ugly. I'm not saying I want to die. I'm not suggesting that death is beautiful. What I'm suggesting is the thought that we are all programmed to believe death is a taboo subject. It is to be avoided. Not talked about. Not seen. Out of sight, out of mind. In fact, death is a reality for all of us. Why not view death with respect instead of fear. As addicts we get close to death. Some get closer than others. When you get close to death, as close as you can, you have a respect for it.

Here's an example. You're at a party. Everybody is having fun, drinking, dancing, and socializing. A group of guys walk in. There's always that one guy, the one everyone fears. As he walks by with his boys, everyone smiles and says hello with absolute fear in their face. They kiss this guy's ass. It's obvious that the people in the room fear this individual, and he knows it. He stares people down as he walks by. He revels in his persona. As he approaches you, he thinks you're another victim. As you make eye contact, he notices that you have no fear in your eyes. You hold your ground and look uninterested, and unimpressed. As he stares into your eyes you can see him start to doubt himself. You notice a subtle quiver in his eyes as he approaches you. He puts his hand out to shake your hand and greet you. He shakes your hand and moves on with his night. That guy is death. He walks the room, looking at all the pathetic souls that bow down to him. But with you, it was different. You didn't disrespect him, nor challenge him. You looked at death like he was any other person. Fearing him would've made you look weak and feel weak. Because of your life experiences, you respect death, not fear him.

After you survive withdrawals you still have a huge mountain to climb. That's all right. I get that. But, surviving withdrawals represents a sense of freedom from the physical and mental misery. Remember going through it but enjoy that you lived. Pain, struggle, and misery are all different now. You now have a sense of peace. When you respect death, and not fear it, that's the difference between living and surviving. It's also the difference between feeling free or feeling trapped. Live free.

Exercise

Talking about withdrawal symptoms and writing them down helped me embrace my shame. I learned that by telling my story it helped others who were going through the same thing. Your story matters. My advice is for you to share your story. It might not help everyone, but it will help someone. That pain and discomfort you endured during withdrawals is the backbone to your future. Generally, when people go through horrific experiences, they'd rather forget those moments. They suppress the memory instead of confronting them. My advice is for you to confront it the best way you can. Going to AA or NA groups could be a wonderful experience for you. Being around those who understand helps immensely. AA and NA groups are an opportunity for you to tell your story. Writing it down is also an option. You could write it down as a story, a poem, or a movie script. Whatever feels therapeutic while doing it is what matters most. Depending on how comfortable you are in front of a camera, you could make a video describing your withdrawal symptoms. Confronting your darkest days creates your brightest ones. From this point forward, make it a point to confront any discomfort that comes your way. Relationships, jobs, and being out in public can be scary when you initially get sober. The more you run from discomfort, the more you'll feel discomfort. It's like trying to outrun your shadow. No matter what you choose, please above all else, tell your story.

Chapter 3
Rehab

For those of you reading this who have been addicts, did you go to rehab, or did you find another way to get through your addiction? I've come across my share of people who did not go to rehab, but managed to become sober. Whether you went to rehab or not, a decision was made. Something happened. Something changed. You were willing to change your situation. For that, I commend you!

On my journey to rehab, I had conflicting emotions. I knew I was supposed to commit to not doing drugs. That addict voice within said otherwise. In fact, not only did it say "No," it said it in a loud and angry tone. I wanted to give rehab a try, but at the same time, I didn't. Going to rehab would give me a chance at beating an evil addiction, and living a better, healthier life. It also represented giving up a life I knew and often enjoyed: the daily game of cat and mouse; the thrill of the chase; getting high. Rehab would end all of that. That evil addiction thought process tried desperately to change my mind.

I overdosed on an airplane going from Detroit,

Michigan to Phoenix, Arizona. I was in the first 24 hours of withdrawal symptoms from opiates and decided to take over 40 muscle relaxers. On top of the muscle relaxers, I had a couple of Klonopin that my heroin dealer gave me for a rainy day. The combination of the three triggered hallucinations, paranoia, and the undeniable withdrawal symptoms. I vaguely remember the incident. Once the plane arrived in Phoenix, the paramedics were waiting. Things got worse once I arrived. It was reported to my family that I would need to be put in an induced coma due to my heart rate reaching dangerous levels. I remember about 2-3 seconds of the incident. I remember seeing my arms and legs tied down to a bed as I was screaming at the top of my lungs and attempting to break free. That's it. Three days later, I woke up and saw my brother sitting by my bedside.

My dad—who had moved to Italy some weeks previously—had flown back to be with me. Dad asked if I was willing to go to treatment. I said yes, reluctantly. (Later, my dad told me I agreed to go, but continued trying to convince him that I would be fine doing it by myself.) I was in a pretty deep fog mentally from the coma, so my thought process was fuzzy. Dad took me to a drug rehab in California. I remember him hugging me goodbye and saying, "You're my son and I will always love you, but if you don't complete this program, never contact me again. I hope the best for you, David." At the time, I didn't realize how hard that was for my dad. He was saying goodbye to a son he no longer knew. He was taking that dreadful plunge into the abyss of fear and chance, not knowing if his son would come out on the other end healthy. I can only imagine what it was like to emotionally commit to completely cutting ties with your own child if they didn't make the effort to get better.

When the addict is first presented with going to rehab, it's usually some form of intervention. Watch the show "Intervention." You can see the 50/50 dilemma going on in the addict's head. Look at their face. See that confusion. That's the voice fucking with their head. You can tell they want to get better. Then you can see the evil voice doing its work, fucking with their mind and telling them to ignore family. During some of the episodes, the addict will leave the room for a cigarette break, trying to take time to think and process this crazy situation. For the non-addicts who watch this show, you probably think, "Just go to rehab. It's not a tough decision. Just do it," not realizing how powerful this little demon within is.

Eventually, many addicts give in to the hope of rehab and say, "Yes, I'll go." However, deep within the addict's mind is that voice saying, "Cool. We'll go, but I will get what I want in the end. I have plenty of time to influence and manipulate you."

Rehabilitation facilities are ready for this dilemma. Ultimately the addict wants better. They are scared, but willing to give it a chance. That voice within has done so much damage that the addict is extremely unsure of ever getting better. That voice is like a CD skipping over and over saying, "This won't work. This won't work. This won't work." It's just relentless. All the while, within the addict, is a sweet innocent kid who just wants happiness.

Envision a little kid standing before a bully with their head down. Not making eye contact, just staring at the ground, but having the courage to tell this bully how they feel. Telling that bully with a soft voice, "I'm going to rehab to get better. To get you out of my life. I think it's going to work." This kid finally has the courage to tell this bully, "I'm not doing this with you anymore."

On route to rehab, the addict wonders if they will actually get the help they need. That's just one of the many hundreds of questions going through their minds. Amazingly, often the addict feels free for the first time in years. That feeling is hope in its purest form. The addict finally feels like "this just might work."

All the while, that bully addiction is beating the kid down over and over, saying, "This won't work. This won't work."

Just by being at a rehab made me feel like I was trying, making an effort, attempting to beat that bully. The single most powerful conflict I've ever endured in life was when I first arrived at rehab. I wanted to fight that bully and he was relentless in his pursuit. Truth was, I had nowhere else to go. Life or death, sink or swim, stand or fall, are the decisions that define our true character. Rehab is that golden opportunity for you to capitalize on that character.

When arriving at rehab, you can't help but think it's familiar. It's like the first day of school, but at a different school you've never heard of. A side of you thinks this is a place of nut jobs, fuckups, and people you don't want to be around. "There is no way there are people here like me, as bad as me, as ugly as me, as destructive as me. No way did any of these people do the things I've done as an addict." Then on the flip side to that, you start to recognize there is a possibility that you can relate to these people. They are possibly like me and know exactly what I'm going through.

When you first arrive, you don't know what to expect. When I went in, I did the meet and greet, the inventory of my clothing, then I was off to the building of withdrawal. The rehab I attended was abstinence-based. I was given water, food, and vitamins. At the time, I thought this rehab was crazy. I thought it was dangerous not to wean me off the heroin. In the end, I came to feel that method was to be the best for me. I had a lot of moments where I hated the methods they were teaching us. I found the negative in everything. On top of hating everyone else, I truly hated myself. Hate was surrounding me in every thought I had. But I still did what was asked of me. I decided to give rehab a try, and when it didn't work out (because *of course* the drugs would win), then at least I would know for sure I was too weak to fight my addiction.

In time, I discovered that I was slowly starting to feel hope again. If there was one thing that helped above all else in rehab, it was time. Rehab can seem depressing at times, but it also provides hope. For years, you convinced yourself not to give sobriety a chance. Once you do, you realize there is hope.

Often in the first days, I was conflicted on what I was doing there, or why should I continue the process. Everyone already knew I was going to fail. That's the evil drug inside your mind. It's always working, trying to get you to return to it. Rehab provides you with the most likely opportunity for success over that voice.

The rehab I attended had nothing but former addicts working there. My ability to bullshit and manipulate were quickly defeated. I hated when my gift for gab was silenced by the knowing laughter of a staff member. I realized I would get nowhere with my usual manipulation. Damn, those hurt. In the beginning, that quick end to my bullshit crushed my ego.

I asked my wife—who was an addict herself—once, "What did you fear most about going to rehab?" She said, "I was frightened of who was going to come out on the other end. I hadn't seen my sober self in 17 years. I had no idea who I really was and if I was going to even like that person." That's a very real and raw truth when faced with going to rehab. The more I thought about it, the more I thought about my own internal fears at the time. I think the fear of not knowing yourself is real. It's in your face, and it becomes a reality when going to rehab. The fear of failure was intense. During my addiction, I had a fake layer of confidence that was driven by opiates. Who was I without that confidence? Who was I without drugs?

At the start of rehab, I disliked everything. I disliked my bed, my room, my roommates, the counselors, the food—everything. What I disliked the most was the perceived politics. I created this idea that the rehab facility didn't truly care about my well-being.

After a month or so, I realized: "This is all my fucking fault. I did this. I created this. I'm here because of my actions. The animosity I have toward rehab stems from my bad choices in life."

Once you can be honest with yourself, you then find yourself buying into the rehab's philosophies. You might still dislike some of the theories, but you give it a chance. You let go of that critical, ignorant, stubborn self. You allow yourself to be open to the possibilities of what might be.

I did not, and do not, follow all of that rehab's philosophies. Rehab is filled with so much useful information. They teach you a variety of things. It was like a buffet of information on addiction. There were some foods I didn't care to eat. Rehab was similar to the way I feel about religion. All religions have beautiful, positive, helpful philosophies on life, and the way to live it. They also have shit that I don't agree with. If I take all the positives from all religions, and practice those things, won't I grow into a better individual? Rehab loaded me with so much positive information, that at times it was overwhelming. I took the positives that the staff taught me and applied it to my life. There were a variety of things that I just didn't agree with. Things that weren't for me were very helpful for others, though. That's what makes rehab beautiful to me.

The greatest thing that happens in rehab is the people. We were all in the same boat. There are countless stories of chaos and anarchy, mischief and madness, success and failure, etc. I talked to people who died and were coming back to life right before my eyes. I met the most unique personalities possible in rehab. I don't meet people like that at work. I don't bump into those kinds of personalities at the grocery store. Rehab is where pure honesty takes place. We were not concerned with judgment from fellow addicts, because everybody else did the same shit. I loved being around blunt, to the point, no filter kind of personalities. I swear I met the funniest people in rehab. And if there's one thing that gets you through rehab, it's the laughter. Laughter was our new drug, and we gravitated to it every chance we got.

Another thing about the people you encounter in rehab is how unattractive they are when they first get there. Don't get me wrong, I'm no supermodel.

I looked like shit when arriving, too! What happens in our minds though is this, "Damn, that mother-fucker looks rough." Within the next couple weeks, you get to know them. Soon, those looks fade into beauty. Next thing you know, you feel honored to have witnessed this person's transformation. We see ourselves in those people. We admire them for go-ing through the struggle. Then for them to come out looking great, hell yeah! That's beautiful.

Now don't get me wrong, you'll meet some fucked up dirty-ass personalities in rehab as well. Some shady, sneaky, stab-you-in-the-back types of people. These people are still in their survival mode that told them that doing some dirty shit was the only way to get through life. Rehab has a little of that high school vibe: cliques, social acceptance, attrac-tive/not attractive. You feel a little of that shit. What's dope about rehab though, you don't care too much. Your "give-a-fuck" meter is at 1 percent and leaning toward zero. You see these things, but don't really care, because your very existence is in question.

What I think is fascinating is this: you get to see the worst in people because that's what they are. They are in the same position as you. They are in their worst position. They question life or death. They are trying to change their ways. You get to meet face-to-face with them. They are a mirror image of what you have become. Don't judge. Don't look at them like you're any better. Truly, they are you. They are famil-iar. Seeing them was an opportunity to see myself.

To pass judgment is nothing more than hypocrisy—and hypocrisy was one of the many things I tried to correct in rehab.

Slowly, the little kid in me that was hope stood up to the hateful doom-saying voice that was my addiction—the bully. Once I believed rehab would work, that's when things started to change. I didn't believe everything they taught me in rehab, but I believed in the process. I believed my life would change for the better. I believed I would not relapse. I believed I would die if I gave in to the bully's voice. Rehab is that tiny sliver of hope; that hope snowballs into belief. Once you believe in yourself and your own capabilities, the sky's the limit.

Having accepted that I—the little boy with hope—can change, it was relatively easy to defeat the addiction. I pictured that bully now as the one sitting on a bench, elbows on his knees, palms covering his weeping eyes. Instead of that little kid laughing at him, or talking shit to him, he puts his hand on the bully's shoulder and embraces him with compassion. That's the power of sobriety.

You will deal with that bully for the rest of your life. His voice will be a part of your thoughts for the remainder of your days. Don't forget that he is, in fact, you. Instead of fighting him with hate and rage, be consistent with love and compassion.

Exercise

Have you ever wanted to spill your heart out to someone so bad that you map out a speech to give them? You then rehearse it in your mind over and over? That's what I suggest you do. Map out your greatest speech that you can say to your addiction. Instead of screaming profanities and cursing at your addiction, give thanks. Compassion in the face of your oppressor will set you free. Thank addiction for all that it showed you. Thank addiction for life's greatest lessons. Tell addiction what you loved most about it. What were the most beautiful qualities addiction had? By giving thanks to your addiction, you are now showing compassion to your once greatest enemy. Embrace him as family by giving him a warm welcome speech that shows love and acceptance versus hate and denial.

Chapter 4

Gravity

Gravity is the force that attracts objects toward the center of the Earth. As a kid, I grew up in the Sierra Nevada mountains, and learned the hard way about gravity's effects, quite often by jumping off of houses, out of trees, off of rocks, etc. We all feel gravity, and we all respect its power and force.

The force of gravity is inevitable. It's also true of any situation that grounds us or brings us back to our reality—and that's a good thing. This is where gravity means something is of great seriousness, magnitude, and importance. I call it "The Fall;" that moment of clarity that we don't like to experience, but it saves us. It's when the gravity of an addict's situation brings them back to Earth with a hard, sudden, often painful crash. The Fall consists of a natural honesty that is pure, real, raw, and organic. That's what makes gravity so pure. It is Nature putting you in check, and not allowing manipulation.

When you're addicted, gravity fucks with you in other ways—pulling you in a variety of directions. While this is happening, you find yourself doing things you wouldn't do sober. I didn't want to do those things to get my drugs, but the addiction gravity forced me to.

I remember numerous times driving to my dealer's house and asking myself, "What am I doing? Just stop. At some point you need to stop this shit, so why not now?" But I'd keep on driving and continue the behavior over and over. Even when I tried convincing myself not to go get the drugs, I'd go get them every time. Heroin made me feel like the drug had its own gravitational pull. When you're addicted to drugs and alcohol it becomes an undeniable force that you can't defy. It's a fucked-up feeling to feel powerless in addiction.

When we make poor choices, we generally know that we shouldn't be doing that. Let me give you an example. When a child lies to an adult for the first time in their life, and gets away with it, they feel an adrenaline rush. That rush of manipulating someone into believing their lie feels exciting. A lot of kids continue lying because they enjoyed the rush. At some point, that rush comes to a crashing halt. They get caught and called out for it and then receive some sort of consequence. That moment where it came to a crashing halt is gravity. That's what I mean by gravity.

I went through a phase during my addiction where I became very judgmental toward the parents of the children I was a counselor to. I would look at them thinking they had no idea what they were doing. I was on a drug-induced high horse that made me believe that since I worked with mentally ill children, I knew everything about parenting. I don't have any children of my own. Drugs made me a very bitter and judgmental man. Once I went to rehab and started to confront these issues, I realized how embarrassed I was by my thoughts and actions. I preached to numerous parents and passed judgment. That embarrassment is gravity. That's the moment where nature caught up with me and checked my attitude.

Throughout my addiction, I was lying to myself every single day. Every time I asked friends if I could borrow money I convinced myself that I would pay that person back. I knew in my heart that they would never see that money again. Every moment of every day was a lie. I was in absolute denial of my addiction.

Think about your daily life as an addict. Some of you reading this didn't try hiding your addiction. Everyone in your life knew you were addicted. When they attempted to get you help, how did you react? Denial of some sort, right? You did and said whatever was necessary to continue feeding the beast. You were lying to yourself and everyone else to feed the addiction. We've all heard that pressure busts pipes. Just like lies, pressure builds and eventually erupts. Our lies catch up and we have no other option but to be honest if we do in fact want to change.

Gravity is a magical moment that is pure honesty. Whether you want to hear it or not, gravity eventually tells you the truth. It's up to you on whether you choose to ignore it or embrace it. If you choose to ignore your problems, then things will get worse and nothing will change. When you embrace honesty by admitting your flaws, you set yourself free from emotional bitterness.

Rehab provides some very challenging moments where you feel the effects of your past actions. Those challenging moments are gravity. When you feel those moments and feel the guilt of your actions, you hurt with rage, hate, bitterness, and guilt. Working through that pain is where you develop a respect for that emotional gravity. By embracing the truth you're letting go of the pain. Tears don't drop without gravity, so let them flow.

When I look back on the last year of my addiction, I can't help but focus on the last two months. I had a progression of situations that signaled the end was near. I felt my internal organs shutting down. I was easily irritable with friends and having arguments with loved ones. Even when I would get high, I was in a tornado of emotional anger toward the world. My life spiraled out of control quickly. I knew death was near, but refused to admit how truly scared I was. That two months leading up to my overdose was gravity letting me know nature was now in control. Whether I lived or died remained to be seen.

A huge part of "The Fall" is recognizing you need help. A lot of times in life we know we need help, but we're too proud to ask for it. Sometimes we struggle to admit defeat. It's like tapping out in wrestling—one of the fighters realizes they can't win and slaps the mat to tell the referee they surrender. Often, that wrestler feels embarrassed or humiliated at having to give in. We feel shame at admitting defeat, when in fact the truth is, our opponent beat us. Yes, we lost, but we lived to fight another day. That loss will teach us a better way, a different strategy. No one likes losing or feeling shame. When you admit you need help, that the addiction is a bigger, better fighter than you, that's just admitting that you need to step your game up. Get help when you need it. The people I admire the most, all admitted defeat, but they got the help they needed to achieve greatness.

Going to rehab presented me with a variety of shitty emotions, but when I look back on it, I knew that I was in a safe environment. The gravity pull of drugs wasn't around. I felt grounded. Rehab brought me back down to Earth—down from that high of madness. I experienced gravity in a new way: now it was a force bringing me back to sobriety. Throughout my six months in rehab, that gravitational force toward sobriety became stronger and stronger. I became more and more in tune with myself and liking what I saw.

My favorite part of The Fall was the recognition of my greatest enemy. I saw him, recognized him, and felt him as my enemy. The crazy part, of course, was that enemy was me: my way of thinking, my personality that I allowed to get out of control.

Even celebrities are subject to addiction's gravity. How many times have we witnessed the rise and fall of someone famous? We watch them come out of nowhere, dance all over our TV/device/movie screens with their talents. They gain fame, money, cars, mansions, and all the other material things. Then you hear they've succumbed to the lure of drugs, or maybe even suffered psychological damage and go into rehab or seek psychological help. Later we discover they were not truly happy being famous. The celebrity speaks about how all of the money and fame couldn't buy them happiness. That's gravity. That's the Fall. That's the realization that you've got problems that are bigger than you.

This journey through life is cause and effect; making mistakes and learning from them. Lose, so you learn how to win. When you've embraced failure as a learning opportunity, then you win. When the gravity of failure hits you, that's when you should be thinking: "It's time to work." That's the moment when you've successfully unlocked one of life's great mysteries. The effect of gravity happens to all of us. Only a few admit its existence. Failure is gravity. Success is always mentored by failure. *Success is a beautiful tree whose roots are made of struggle.*

Exercise

For this exercise, I want you to consider the power of honesty. My theory with gravity is that the truth will come out eventually, and everything that you're doing wrong will come to a crashing halt. Be honest with yourself about the gravity moments that hit you when you were sobering up. Identify the top 3 situations in your life that gravity came crashing down on you. You're most likely going to think of the biggest ones first. Once you've done that, now start to think about all the little things that you've done wrong in your life—where gravity got you. When you identify these situations, be honest about your emotions. The purpose in doing this is to identify the behaviors you once had, and how they came to a crashing halt. When you think about these things, you're more likely to recognize if you're currently doing anything that might end in gravity. The more you identify what led to gravity getting you, then the more likely you are to not encounter it ever again.

Chapter 5

Searching

What do you want out of life today, tomorrow, and in the future? Are you willing to search and put in the work necessary to achieve it? Are you living or surviving? As addicts, we search in all the wrong places for all the wrong things. In sobriety, if you search for a healthier lifestyle, you're going to find it.

Before we delve into the world of searching and researching, remember the importance of patience and trusting the process. When you were born, someone tended to you. You were dependent on that someone. You became familiar with them. You watched them, and by doing so, you learned how to survive. You learned how to crawl and tipped over at times. Then you learned how to walk and stumbled at times. When you learned how to run and then to sprint, you fell hard at times. That's the process. Everything that you search for that's worth something has hardship in it, and with that hardship comes a lesson.

What makes life after addiction enjoyable is searching for what you want. Obviously, you want to create a lifestyle that will keep you away from drugs. Going to your old dope dealer's house to say hello and see how he's been isn't a smart start. Going to the bar, or clubs, isn't wise either. So, the questions are, what do you need to do to get a job; eat; find shelter; get healthy? These are some of the basic things that need to be tended to right off the bat. But really, your next question should be what you would like to do for happiness. Boredom can easily lead to relapse. Ask the questions and find the answer. Questions mean you need to search for the answers.

What should drive your search is curiosity about how you can deal with sobriety. I was always told that curiosity was a bad thing. I think I heard that speech about curiosity killing the cat about a thousand-plus times. I believe I was told that so frequently because I was always curious about risky things that could cause bodily harm (like alcohol and drugs). When you find sobriety, you're searching for a better way to deal with it. When you're curious about living a happy life, and curious about how to get it, you will find it. Curiosity is beautiful because you find that the possibilities are endless.

When you search for information, and have the willingness to find answers, then you learn and grow as a person. We all have curiosity. Think about how many times you've been curious about something and you convinced yourself not to pursue it, mainly because you fear it won't go well. You fear you'll fail. You fear the humiliation of getting it wrong. Fuck that! When you're curious about something you care about, something worth fighting for, then do it. No fear. No regrets. As an addict, you were as close to death as you could possibly get. You won't die trying to achieve a happier life. Never forget the importance of failure. When you're an addict, you've already failed more than most people can imagine.

I loved searching for bad things as a kid, but I hated getting caught. I'd get as close to danger as possible. I discovered the greatest joys stemmed from the greatest risks. I was generally willing to do dangerous things to prove a point to the neighborhood kids and show my lack of fear. I just wanted to search, discover, and understand as much about life as possible. Searching and experiencing life felt like the most natural thing to do.

Growing up in a small town didn't meet my needs. I wanted more, I yearned for more, and searched for whatever it was that was driving me. I've met a lot of people who grew up in a small town and had no ambition to move to a big city. I've met a lot of big city people who had no ambition to move to a small town. If you don't explore, or don't search, then how will you ever know what it is that you truly like or dislike?

When I graduated high school and went off to college, I was exposed to a variety of things I had never seen: cultures, religions, beliefs, the list goes on and on. I loved meeting new people because they opened me to new ideas and explored a variety of interests.

Later in life when I became addicted, I would search for things that made me happy without drugs. The problem was, I was still using while doing this searching. I wanted to be sober, I wanted to be happy without drugs, but I couldn't stop using. I wanted to run away from myself. It was like a game of hide and seek with my nemesis, but my nemesis happened to be me. I found it fascinating to dislike myself so much. Then love aspects of myself.

Sobriety forces you to look deep within yourself. It's a journey into the unknown. That's what makes sobriety so much fun. You're finally willing to search for the real you. I didn't know who I was before or during addiction. Sobriety pushed me to have a better understanding of who I am.

I got a job opportunity in Mississippi and moved there. I yearned for change, had good intent, but never followed through on changing my behavior. This was a repetitive thought process for years. I wanted to move to foreign countries, hide out in the woods, and live off the land. Moving from state to state was an attempt to run away from my issues.

When I was "just" an alcoholic, before the heavy drug use, I was trying to get a job working with kids in the Bahamas. This was my attempt at treating my alcoholism. At the time, I was in the Midwest working with emotionally disturbed youth. These kids had gone through horrific situations in their life.

So, my big plan was to take the skills I learned in that job, and move. I was getting done with college and the world seemed open to exploration. I figured there are kids with issues everywhere and I wanted to help. Subconsciously, I think my plan was to go somewhere that drinking wouldn't be such an escape. I needed to go somewhere that was surrounded by beauty. I assumed there would be no need for rehab in the Bahamas.

I was at a night club one night in Kansas City, and I met this guy who was from Jamaica. I chopped it up with him about life in Jamaica and I told him my big plan. He laughed—not unkindly—but because he knew it was a silly idea. He told me that Americans have these wondrous ideas of saving the world in other countries, forgetting that these other countries are not like America. The Bahamas, Jamaica, and countless other countries, have their own set of issues. He told me that the kids in Jamaica were mainly in trouble for stealing from tourists. They stole because they were hungry. They stole to help provide for their family. It was not because they were bad kids, they stole for survival. This guy said, "If you want to go make a difference over there with the kids, go change our government first."

In that moment, I was turned off at the idea. Going to the Bahamas was not about helping others, it was about the great escape.

My next big plan was Honduras. I was deeply saddened when Lisa "Left-eye" Lopes from the group TLC, died in Honduras. I remember admiring her for going down there to the retreat with natural healer Dr. Sebes. I loved hearing interviews with her about what she was doing there. She explained about her personal self-growth and learning healthier ways to live. I could see myself doing the same thing. I wanted to do more with my life and the route she was going appealed to me. The more I researched the place, the more I loved the thought of changing aspects of my lifestyle. Once again, I was trying to escape myself. I never went there, either.

My alcohol consumption continued; it made me feel euphoric, but also made me depressed. People who drink love to forget that alcohol is a depressant.

I've watched people do this game of hide and seek many times. Say that they want change, and think moving out of town is the answer. I like that they're trying. I admire that. What happens is they move, sober up, and succeed for a couple months. Then when they get that itch—that undeniable itch—they go right back to their addiction. Sometimes they go back to their hometown as an excuse to use again. They do that and get right back in the same struggle. Months later, they end up wanting to move again to go sober up. The ultimate issue with this is the psychological help that is needed to treat their addiction is being ignored.

Being able to look back and evaluate where I went wrong as a youngster was vital to my sobriety.

When you come to your senses and realize you're a full-blown addict, you ask questions like, "How did I get to this point in my life? Why did I think this was a good route to go? When did this all go sideways? Where was I in my life? What was I doing or not doing?" One of the most significant moments for me was answering those questions honestly. It takes a lot of time, a lot of self-reflecting, and a lot of patience. When these questions are answered, you discover a different you that you had no idea existed. It's a beautiful experience because it proves to you that this does get better, you can beat this addiction and you do matter.

I've been told on many occasions not to think about the past, don't dwell on the past, just focus on the present. But I think of withdrawals every day. At some point in my day, mainly in the morning, I think about how ugly life once was. By doing this, I appreciate and show gratitude toward myself. I've worked hard in my sobriety to find this gratitude. I love what I've accomplished, but I do this by remembering my failures.

Searching for a better you will be a life-long journey. It's a journey that's filled with beautiful lessons. Sobriety is an eye-opening experience if you allow it to be. It's not depressing like you would think.

In your internal and physical journey to search for more, choose wisely. If you go searching for anything bad, you're more likely to find just that. If you search for good, clean, healthy things every single day, then you will find just that. Search for happiness. Search for love.

Travel if you can. Go places you've never gone in your town, your country, your world. Obviously, don't go places that might trigger you, but go on an adventure. I've been to around 40 different U.S. states and 6 different countries. There's so much out there to see. With all that I encountered in my travels, what I found to be the most impactful truth was discovering when I was getting closer to myself versus running from myself. Travelling for pleasure is a beautiful experience of searching and learning more about your true character, while travelling for the purpose of avoidance gets you stuck in a self-destructive loop. Now that I'm sober, I get to see things clearly. I advise you to be adventurous. Be safe of course, but adventurous.

I've watched other addicts in recovery try new things, like going to a gym and joining classes, even though they're uncomfortable with being around people while exercising. I've seen addicts in recovery go on hikes with groups of people they never would've associated with before. In recovery, we're fragile at first. Those little things are scary moves to make. Searching takes practice. Making an effort to do things you don't want to do, but deep inside you do want to, is hard.

This book is an accumulation of all the researching I have done to master my own sobriety. It doesn't mean I'm a black belt in sobriety, it just means that

I mastered the art of my own sobriety. I encourage you to do the same thing, search for the very best you.

Exercise

Write out a list of things that you've always been curious about but never tried. Set a date within the next week to accomplish your goal. If you say "within a year," then you're more likely to procrastinate. If you set the goal within a week, it's fresh in your mind and you're more likely to achieve it. Once you've done it, then make sure this becomes a weekly occurrence. Once you're comfortable challenging yourself, then you know you're ready for your next goal. Start out small.

I struggled with social anxiety when I first got out of rehab. I would go to the grocery store and try my best to make eye contact with people and say hello. Not in a creepy way but a subtle way. I know that sounds small, but at the time I was very vulnerable. That was a big step for me. As you write your list, think about things that other people would perceive as small, but for you it's a frightening thought. The more you practice these things, the more you become comfortable with them.

Chapter 6

Confronting Yourself

When you're faced with rehab, interventions, or fixing your issues, you have no choice but to confront your addiction. Confronting and dealing with every issue that you face dictates your success or not, and a potential relapse, or not. Confronting yourself honestly, with integrity should be in your daily thoughts for the remainder of your life.

Honesty is the most important element of this process. When you're an addict, your ability to be honest with yourself is gone. Every move you make as an addict is to obtain your drug of choice by any means necessary. Being honest and doing the right thing would get in the way of obtaining this goal.

My favorite moment while I was in rehab was when I came to the realization that I had been lying to myself. From then on I didn't care who liked or disliked me. I considered my friends and family all gone, and I was starting a new life of complete honesty. It's really frightening to accept that you have nothing. Everything you've known is gone.

Now to be honest—since we're talking about

being honest—there was a bit of self-pity going on there. I had a variety of emotions in rehab, and self-pity was absolutely one of them. Because of my extreme personality, I convinced myself that none of my friends or family would ever talk to me again. I believed that this was the pain I deserved and the pain I needed. I believed I needed to endure this pain to appreciate my sobriety. The next step was accepting that I couldn't change what I had done, but I could control my future if I took the right steps in rehab.

Before I went to rehab, I called an old friend who had struggled with alcoholism. I told him, "I think I can do this on my own and I'm just seeking advice from those who have gone through similar situations."

He told me he would love to talk and give me the advice I needed. He asked me if I had tried kicking the heroin and pills on my own.

I said, "Yes, about 40 - 50 times at least."

He said, "Wow! How's that going for you?"

I replied, "Not good, but…."

He stopped me. "No, your way of dealing with this, sucks. Your ability to take control of this sucks. Basically, you suck at life right now—and that's okay. But if you don't accept the fact that you suck at getting sober, then you will continue to lose this battle."

I hated every word. It seemed to me his mouth was spewing pure bullshit in my ears and I didn't have time for this whack-ass advice. I politely got off the phone with him, and within in the next month I overdosed and ended up going to rehab.

Confronting what he said to me was hard, because he was 100 percent correct. To confront yourself and admit that you suck at this getting clean thing fucked my brain up in necessary ways. I'm an egomaniac who has always believed I need to handle shit on my own. No one can help me but me. Holy shit, how wrong I was. That was another example of the difference between arrogance and confidence. My arrogance was out of control while I was under the influence. Sobering up and confronting these issues enabled me to be humble and confident.

When my addiction started, it was the end of 2005 going into 2006. I had moved back to the West Coast to help my mother with her declining health. I have fond memories of my mother. She was the only person on this Earth I felt I could call, ask any question, and she would have the answer. My mom was a genius and a fascinating conversationalist. She was a high school teacher and very respected in the community. I had my mother as a teacher in high school and she was awesome at what she did. Mom was very respected by the students, faculty, and the parents. The parents were a problem because they asked her not to retire, to teach one more year (and one more, and one more…). They wanted their kids to have her as a teacher and then her letters of recommendation to get their kids into the top colleges. Had my mother just taken some time off from teaching to focus on her ailing knees, then she never would have fallen and broken her hip. That was the start of her decline. After the hip healed, she needed one surgery after the other.

She developed an array of health issues that required numerous surgeries—and a massive amount of medications. She was taking a variety of pain pills, Norco, Morphine, Vicodin, etc. Then she was taking Xanax for anxiety, Ambien and Lunesta for sleep, and 20 other pills for an array of other ailments. My mother was always sharp and on point, but her doctors convinced her the medications were all right to take. She became addicted to those pills—which she never admitted to. She didn't like being under the influence of anything, but she became addicted because the doctors told her they were okay.

I would swipe pain pills from her Dr. Feelgood shoebox of medications. I would tell myself, "I won't take them often. I'll be good. I'll just take them here and there." My behavior just got worse and worse.

My mother died in 2008. At that point, I was two years into a full-blown addiction. When she died, I no longer had access to the pills. Black market, here I come! Once the pills became too expensive, I transitioned to heroin. I tried the needle-thing but didn't like the possibility of having track marks and getting caught. How do you keep your addiction quiet if you've got track marks? I was a dragon chaser. I would put the heroin on a sheet of aluminum foil, use the lighter under the foil, and inhale the smoke as the black tar slid down the foil. I can still taste it as I write this—it was nasty. Similar to alcohol though, that taste was delicious because of its effects.

Once my mom died, heroin became my new love. I used drugs so I wouldn't have to confront the grief I felt. I would throw myself little pity parties that she was gone, but I didn't really address how much I missed my mom.

A year or so later, my sweet cousin passed away at the age of 26. She was diagnosed with clinical depression. She was one of those personalities that I call kindergarten teachers—you know the type--always nice and have the spirit of an angel. That's how she was. At the time of her passing she was going to school to become a psychologist. When she was found in her apartment, she was holding a cross in the palm of her hand, never letting go of hope.

Instead of confronting my grief, I threw myself a pity party again. Poor me. I cried as I stood over my cousin's casket, thinking that it should've been me lying there. Why the fuck was I still alive? On the morning of my cousin's funeral, I took in between 40 - 50 40mg Oxycontin pills. They didn't seem to affect me at all. My tolerance grew stronger and stronger, so I continued to feed the beast.

After my first two months in rehab, I started coming to my senses. I was able to identify the issues that enabled me to get worse and worse. The true test was confronting my mother's death. Admitting I was stealing pills from my mother while she was dying was even more difficult.

Then I considered the patterns all around me: my mother passed away, my cousin passed away, and one of the kids I coached overdosed. What the fuck? Should I get mad at the pharmaceutical companies? Should I make excuses for all of this? When I confronted myself and was honest, the answer was no. I had done this to myself. It was up to me to correct the behavior. I had to hit it head on and admit to my role in every facet of that fucked up situation. Confront the shit out of all of it. Own it!

Confronting your insecurities can be your biggest challenge. Think about your insecurities in a relationship, the job you hate, friendships that smell of deceitfulness. Once you recognize these situations as hurtful toward your growth, then you're able to take the deep plunge into the ocean of insecurities. We convince ourselves that these situations are going to work themselves out and everything will be good again. What does your instinct tell you? Don't mistake your insecurities for instinct. Your gut tells you to "get out." Your mind tells you to keep trying. Think about break-ups. You want to stay, and you want it to be good again. It just never gets better. Confronting the emotional battle of saying "goodbye" is the toughest part. When you sober up and confront your insecurities, saying goodbye becomes normal. It feels great to say goodbye to the bad things in your life and you don't feel those overwhelming insecurities anymore.

One break-up I experienced was strictly because I wasn't in control. She cancelled me, which crushed my drugged-out ego. I begged for her to come back, so I could then break-up with her and feel the sense of control. I didn't really care about *her*, I only cared about my insecurities. She made the right decision, and I admire her for that. When you're under the influence, you want to be right, you want to be in control, you want what you want, when you want it. You expect instant gratification. It's a part of your existence. Your insecurities during a break-up are nothing but that, insecurities.

I sometimes look at my insecurities the same way I view guilt. It's good to admit you have those emotions. It's good to show that you care, but it can be destructive if you don't have a grasp on it. I made a bad decision one night and felt guilty the next day. My friend said this to me, "Guilt shows that you care about your bad decision-making, but it also shows that you're dwelling on something you have no control over. You can't go back to last night and change it. It's done. It's gone. Learn from it, but don't sit and feel guilty about something from your past. It's pointless. Guilt is basically a pointless emotion." Guilt shows that you have a heart, but letting it consume you is pointless. Insecurities are similar. I feel them every day. I just don't allow them to consume me. I accept them as a neighbor I only see in passing.

Confronting my ego has been interesting. To be 100 percent honest with yourself is to admit your flaws, and therefore admitting you're human. We try so hard to dress our personality up to impress others, when that behavior convinces us to live a lie. Ego can help build confidence, but it can be a cover-up for insecurities. When you can be honest with yourself and recognize these insecurities, you find yourself feeling free. When I openly admit to people my insecurities, I feel free, honest, and above all, respected. You can see in other's faces that they respect you for that. Some try to play it off like they don't identify with you, but they do. They're just not ready to be honest yet. Being confident with yourself, and graceful at the same time, is the ultimate goal.

One of the many things I needed to confront was my jealousy of others. I found myself jealous of a lot of people and disgusted with myself. I was jealous of sobriety. I was jealous of those who could drink a beer or two, then call it a night. I was jealous of people who had a sense of confidence without the necessity of drugs or alcohol. I was jealous of people who didn't allow fear to hold them back from success. I'd get jealous of other people smiling. I'd get jealous of anyone having fun.

My jealousy of others was a direct result of how truly miserable I was. The jealousy was one thing, but my judgment of others was a whole different thing. Fascinating how someone who's addicted to drugs has the audacity to judge others, but I did. In my mind, anyone with nice material things, were materialistic. Anyone in a healthy relationship, cheaters. Anyone with money, they stole it. Anyone talking, they're lying. Confronting yourself on your own disgusting behaviors and thoughts is a frightening experience.

I've been fighting with fear since life began. It's an emotion with an extremely fine line. We feel fear every day on very small levels. I don't walk into traffic because of fear. I know to stop, and let cars go by before I cross the road. When we see police on the freeway, most of us slow down before even checking our speedometer. When we cook food, we proceed with caution because there is a fear of hurting ourselves or burning down the house.

Fear also holds us back from prospering. When I was a kid, I loved baseball, but wasn't any good at it. The other kids I played with were good. Instead of challenging myself, I allowed my fear of failure to overwhelm me and keep me stagnant. It's as if my evil side was telling me to know my place and keep that bench warm. All of us have had moments in our lives where fear dictated whether we had the courage to do something or not. "I fear failure and being judged for it. So why try at all? I'm good where I'm at." Those are the most common fears within us. The most successful people in the world overcame those fears. They found something within themselves that said, "No more worrying. I will succeed."

Addiction is regarded as a mental weakness by society. I find it to be my greatest strength. My fear of life as a sober man was so strong that suicide almost had me. I just didn't believe there was happiness after the taste of opiates. I've seen people come out of thirty-day treatment facilities and look absolutely miserable: depressed; unsure; straight fear in their eyes. I thought, "If that's what sobriety looks like, then I'll ride this addiction thing out until it kills me." That's what fear did to me. I was lost as an addict because I didn't think it was possible to be sober and happy.

When you first go to rehab, you have nothing but fear and doubt. It's fascinating how quickly we forget how successful we were at getting drugs. We would go above and beyond. I realized that with the same determination, I could be sober. Why can't I be successful in sobriety? Why can't I be happy in sobriety? I found success in addiction and now I'll find success in sobriety. This is a daily fight with fear and doubt.

Fear will keep you down. Fear will eat at your soul as if it's starving. Fear will keep you questioning a better life. Fear will hold you back from whatever life you thought you wanted. Fear will never allow you to have what you want. Fear hates you and wants you to lose. Fear will bully you over, and over, and over again. And it will keep on winning until that one magical moment happens when you've lost your shit and can't take it anymore. You no longer care about failure, embarrassment, and loss. You ball up your fist on that punk-ass bully Fear and knock the fuck out of him. You finally fight back. You have one objective for your day—to obtain your happiness. You will do whatever it takes to achieve this goal, and nothing will stand in your way. That's how you face fear, you fight back.

I feel fear every morning I wake up. Every morning I listen to music on my phone and reflect on withdrawals. Some people think it's unhealthy to think back on the past, especially the ugly things. Facing those fears—demons if you will—is a beautiful reminder of how good life is now. Each day I know I will experience fear. I fear that I'll forget how beautiful my life is, or forget to be grateful today. What I fear most of all is not taking advantage of sobriety. All of us in recovery should be dead because of our addictions. I fear forgetting that. I now allow fear to be a driving force to success versus failure.

One of my major issues is that I'm a people pleaser. I want people to be happy with me. I want to help others. As a kid I was gullible, easily persuaded by others. When others said I couldn't do something, or that I couldn't succeed in something, I would either let their comments rule over me or I would get offended and prove them wrong. It took a long time for me to realize how other people's opinions and comments affected me. Unfortunately, there were times that I didn't follow through with a goal I desired because I feared that other people's discouraging comments were correct. Truth is, that's their fears, not mine. I got my own demons, why should I be affected by yours? Think about how many times someone put their fears on you—meaning they feared you succeeding, so they talked shit to you. They wanted to beat you down because of their fears and insecurities.

I experience fear every single day because it's an unavoidable emotion. My goal is to eliminate the fear of how I react to others. How I deal with my own emotions dictates my success for every single moment of every single day. Once I make a variety of good decisions each moment, then I'm more likely to not allow fear to dictate my day.

After my first year in college, I questioned my ability to play football at the next level. My fear stemmed from watching these teammates with a massive amount of talent. I doubted myself and feared I had nothing to offer. I was relevant in high school but not at the college level. After that first year, my old high school coach asked me what happened in the last year? What he was asking was where did my drive go? He saw the lack of drive in my eyes. My greatest quality was my work ethic. His question turned to comments of encouragement. My attitude changed that day. I *could* play at the college level. My fear was holding me back. I immediately started working out again and changed my attitude.

Two weeks before heading back to college for my second year, I fell out of a tree landing on rocks that tore my ACL. I tried toughing it out, went back to college, and went to practice as if nothing had happened. During practice, the quarterback handed me the ball, and as I went to make a cut, my knee gave out. The doctor said my ACL was torn 100 percent and my MCL was torn 95 percent. I had reconstructive knee surgery that took nine months to rehab. I played four years of college football after that injury. I didn't allow fear to dictate my belief in myself.

Two years after that accident in the tree, my friends and I went through a national park while doing mushrooms. When we came upon an oak tree, we decided that was a perfect hang-out spot. I paused, felt fear, but quickly decided that fear holds you back so get in the fucking tree.

As I was climbing the tree, my best friend noticed a look in my eye and said, "Holy shit man. This is the first time you've been in a tree since the accident?"

I replied, "Yeah it is."

My friends looked at one another. One said, "He conquers his fears, all the time."

My sense of pride blossomed that day. I know climbing in a tree sounds bland, but in those moments, you rethink your situation. You think about that nine months of rehab. Unfortunately, people don't generally recognize those moments as vital opportunities for growth. Recognize your fears, face them, and fight.

Take this book for instance. I fear that people won't receive it the way I want. I fear people will judge me for my outlook on sobriety, and think my philosophies are weak. I fear vulnerability will beat me down and I won't ever finish this book. If you are reading this, then you know I conquered those fears.

Confronting your fears is a monster, but confronting your habits and routines is a different level. As you work toward addressing yourself, you discover aspects where you are set in your ways—which makes you complacent. You're stuck in one way of thinking and not allowing yourself to be open-minded. When you're complacent, you allow that voice to influence you to make bad choices. Next thing you know, you're convincing yourself to do the very least you can to keep going in the same direction.

My daily way of living is pretty set: I shower, eat, exercise, etc. I keep things around the house clean—to the point where my wife will look at how strategic I place my belongings, and then mess them up intentionally. We both laugh, because it's her way of saying, "Relax a little bit." If I was set in those ways, then that shit she just did would cause a fight. I realize some of my idiosyncrasies should take a break, and it's good to be reminded occasionally.

Being able to confront these things has been a beautiful blessing for me. I like me, I like the way I am, but I also like that I can change. Sometimes society convinces us that we have to be an adult and believe in one way of being and thinking. I love being open-minded and willing to learn new things. My beliefs on my sobriety will alter at times. As long as the objective is sobriety, then I'm on board with whatever. That evil little voice within yourself is waiting for you to slip up. What happens when you get set in your ways is that you're basically saying you know best and there's no other way. Does that behavior make you feel good? If you feel good and you know you're being good to yourself, then beautiful. If you're doing it out of bitterness and arrogance, then you just unlocked the forbidden door to the person you're trying to keep out.

Confronting every aspect of my being has been the most mature decision I've ever made. I absolutely love me, but I can get better. I'm uneducated on a variety of levels and I know that. Confronting the bad I see within myself is an aspect of honesty, integrity, and maturity. It's tough to admit when you're wrong. But like everything else, it takes practice.

Confronting that voice, that demon, that ugly side to you, is not a matter of muscle, it's a matter of mind. That voice will never leave. It is a part of you forever. I look at facing your addiction the same way Dr. Martin Luther King Jr. looked at a non-violent approach. So often we are faced with adversity and our instinct is to physically or verbally act out. Dr. King chose love over rage and hate. Why can't I take the same approach to my addictive personality? I just need to be courageous and confront it. When we confront our addiction correctly, we find ourselves free from the misery. Drugs tried killing the real me. Sobriety tried killing the addict in me. Neither of them succeeded. Truth was, I needed to experience the evil within to discover the good.

Confronting both your good and evil, is one of life's great mysteries. It's not just an addict thing, that's a life thing.

Practicing identifying the difference between your insecurities and your instinct. The greatest way to practice it is by being authentically honest.

Exercise

Make a list of the people you need to confront and make amends with. Let them know how sorry you are for your actions.

If you stole money from a friend, make an effort to meet with them, tell them your story and make amends. Tell them about the emotions you went through when reality came crashing down on you. By doing this they will get to hear what you went through when you recognized what you had been going through. This can be a very impactful moment for you and for them. Expressing these experiences shows strength within yourself and a willingness to accept responsibility for your actions. Please note: If you think you are putting yourself in a dangerous situation by going to talk to a friend who you wronged, then don't do it. Make sure they are willing to hear you out. This can and will be the most powerful opportunity for you to express your profound apologies to those you hurt the most. This exercise is the most nerve-wracking one you'll do, but hands down the most rewarding.

Chapter 7

Perspective

My perspective has always been driven by my feelings. I'm aware that my thought process on a moment-by-moment basis needs perspective, which has changed since I sobered up. In fact, it changed dramatically. When you're under the influence and in the depths of addiction, you generally don't give a fuck about anything except feeding your addiction. Your perspective on life is selfishness and bitterness. Sobriety offers you an opportunity to have a healthy perspective toward your future. In recovery, you re-examine life. What makes it exciting is that it's a second chance. You get to start a whole new you. What are some of the things you always wanted to do or be? Your perspective on work, friendships, relationships, and finances is totally up to you. Perspective is the way in which you view your future of sobriety.

It's not just one day at a time for me, it's every moment and every decision that matters. Each decision I make dictates my success with sobriety. By having a good perspective, I increase my success at life. My extreme personality can now be my greatest asset. I have a bucket of bucket lists and intend to achieve every item on it.

One of my favorite human beings who got me thinking about perspective was Steve Irwin the Crocodile Hunter. I loved his enthusiasm and infectious energy! He would pick up one of the world's most venomous snakes, look it in the face, and tell it how beautiful it was. That shit used to crack me up. A lot of people dislike and fear snakes. Not good old Steve. He thought they were beautiful, real "rippers." Irwin also adored crocodiles. He'd wrestle them, hug them and tell them how beautiful they were. This man loved all animals and was extremely passionate about what he did for work. He would explain to the audience why these creatures were so fascinating and what made them unique. With that, he sold me! I looked at these creatures through his perspective and agreed with him.

If Steve Irwin could get me to see venomous animals as beautiful, then what holds me back from changing my perspective on my recovery? That's what makes people like Steve Irwin so special for humanity. If I choose to look at my addiction from a positive point of view, then maybe I can deal with my problem with compassion. That's what ended up happening over these years of sobriety. My perspective on recovery has changed to one of compassion, enthusiasm, and love.

One of the key factors that I found very important was to be open-minded. This means you're allowing yourself to be open to information. I have absolutely loved my years of sobriety because I have researched, listened, and opened my eyes and heart to any information that will help me maintain my sobriety. During my years of addiction, I was like a teenager, I was sure I knew everything. In sobriety I realized how I knew nothing. My perspective on being open-minded helped me re-establish a variety of skills that helped me maintain my sobriety.

When alcohol entered the picture, my self-esteem crashed. The older I got, the more I drank to feel less sorry for myself. Once I got into the pain pills, then I thought I was the king of the world. Then the heroin was like I made a deal with the Devil. I would still daydream of a happy life while under the influence. They were nothing more than fantasy. I had no idea how dark my perspective had become. I thought the world around me was extremely ugly.

One of the best things that happened to me in rehab was when I started to get my logic back. Then my ability to daydream came back. With that came a stronger sense of hope. I was then able to give sobriety a better chance. I knew my perspective changed when I started to accept the things I had done while under the influence. My life with a logical state was like building my dream home. Some moments in rehab can make you think long and hard about your perspective; like death, for instance.

While I was addicted to drugs and alcohol, I was too numb to experience the pain of losing family members. I refused to confront my true feelings and the natural process we must go through when dealing with grief and loss. My perspective toward grief and loss as a sober man is to endure the natural stages that we all go through. Once I've done that, I feel it's best to honor the dead. I look to better myself and my life in their memory. That's what helps me through the loss of a loved one. In my sobriety, I've lost a few friends and I dealt with it by practicing what I preach. It was as if the autumn leaves of self-destruction and self-pity fell. All I needed to do was go rake up the yard and accept that seasons change.

Drugs had such a lock on me that my emotions were influenced by drugs and alcohol every day—my thoughts were consumed by getting high daily. When I was in rehab, I made a vow to practice thinking positive thoughts to start my day off. I would move my negative emotions to tears of joy, if I could.

Since I left rehab, I've learned to do exactly what's best for me, before I do anything for anyone else. I come first. It's not done in a selfish way. I have to have a greater understanding of my thoughts and emotions before I commit to action. That's how I keep myself clean, by creating the space to understand the reason I am doing things.

I practice being a better man every day. Because of that, I find myself pretty damn happy. I love life and I appreciate that recovering from my addiction is the guiding force that set all of this in motion. My perspective on addiction is all about channeling my energy for a greater me. I've noticed that my attitude toward rules has changed in sobriety: I don't care about the law, I care about being morally sound. With that attitude I sound rebellious, which is funny, but I'm not being rebellious at all. I'm doing everything I can to strengthen my character and avoid potential issues.

While in rehab for six months, I questioned my existence on this Earth. I believed that people who didn't have addiction issues were better than me. I looked at them as a more complete person than I was—better balanced. I assumed they automatically had a beautiful way of looking at the world.

When I reached sobriety, I realized that my assumptions about non-addicted people just wasn't the case. There are a lot of ugly people with ugly-ass personalities, and they don't have addiction issues. I spent six months working on finding a better me, and these people with no addiction issues don't seem to have spent any time at all thinking through their lives and choices. What was up with that? The answer to that is: that's none of my business. Other people's behaviors should not dictate my emotions. My sole responsibility is to focus on myself and my sobriety.

I felt spiritually lost. After some deep thinking, I was able to recognize that *I am just a human being*. And, just as shocking, those other non-addicted people are just human beings as well. We're just trying to find our way, and at times, we get lost and caught up in poor life choices. Practice being better than that.

In the first year of sobriety, I was sensitive to pain. From my years of football and all of my sporadic behaviors, I was in a lot of pain. I heard a doctor say that most opiate addicts struggle with pain in the first year. When you spend years numbing yourself with drugs, then it takes a while to regain a healthy pain tolerance. Now that I'm sober, it's going to take time to allow my body––and pain tolerance––to re-adjust to life after drug abuse. I've had the flu twice since sobriety and found it to still be miserable, but not like it used to be. It's different now. I will never forget how miserable withdrawal symptoms were and because of that I'm able to endure pain with a different perspective.

When I encounter emotional pain, it's the same story as the flu. It is miserable—there's no denying that—but it's not as bad as life once was. I'm not suggesting that dealing with physical and emotional pain is easy, I'm merely encouraging others to look at what they've endured while confronting their addiction issues. Hardship has a key ingredient, it's hard. If you've gone through a lot of hardship, then you are, in fact, tough. That's what makes addicts so beautiful to me: their ability to adapt, their willingness to survive, and their strength to endure pain.

Unfortunately, we get wrapped up in thoughts of negativity. So those things you should be grateful for become muddy and unseen. Clean that shit up. You're in control of those thoughts, so you have the power to keep that muddy water clean. Too often we lose sight of the little things. Look at life through the eyes of a child. I watch my grandson, and every day all that matters to him is to play, have fun, eat when he's hungry, and take naps. He looks at life as entertainment, where I look at life as serious responsibilities. It's up to me to change my attitude. I obviously don't have the luxury of playing all day, or eat when I feel like it, but I do have the power to change my perspective. What children remind us is to stop thinking life is so serious. We can take a more simplified approach. When we chose to look at our five senses every morning, we look at life differently. When we look outside and appreciate nature, we look at life differently. When we think about work and choose to be grateful for having a job, we look at life differently.

I want to suggest something that helps tremendously with perspective: how you perceive time. At what point in life did time become valuable to you? I ask because I believe my outlook on time changed when I came out of my haze in rehab. I could hear time ticking in my head. I mean that in a good way. This life-altering addiction punched me in the face and screamed, "Time's ticking away!" That's when the shift happened. That's when my perspective changed. Time now meant more to me than it ever had before. In fact, I don't remember thinking time mattered at all. The most powerful question you can ask yourself, is, what does time mean to you now that you survived addiction?

Feeling the emotion of gratitude is the bridge between mental chaos and peace of mind. The single most challenging aspect to sobriety is your mindset. Day in, and day out, you're faced with adversity. Maintaining abstinence is a daily battle that takes mental effort. When you practice gratitude every day, that feeling of being in a fight dissipates. You're not fighting every day, you're appreciating every day! Gratitude is calming. Gratitude is peace of mind. It reminds you that the mental chaos of addiction is nothing more than thoughts, not actions. Thoughts are like infomercials. They can be interesting, but they can also be repetitive gibberish. Gratitude helps those thoughts become positive, which will lead to positive actions. Gratitude equals love, and as you know, love conquers all.

Love is always the greatest force on this earth. The greatest way for me to feel a natural high—tap into my natural dopamine reserve—is to feel love. It takes effort from you to change your perspective on this crazy world. When you turn away from addiction, research what truly makes you happy. Material things won't be the answer. Your changed perspective from the craziness of addiction will transform when you learn to love yourself. Only you hold the key to unlocking your new perspective. This isn't a one-shot deal, this is daily.

Remember that your thoughts start it all; they dictate your emotions. Negative thoughts equal negative emotions. Your emotions generate how you feel mentally and physically. Practice loving something about you: teeth, eyes, lips, maybe a certain way you look at things. Whatever it is, identify it. Love it. Embrace it. Feel it. The more you practice those thoughts, the better you get. Create thoughts of love as often as possible. Your perspective on everything in this world will be a part of this process. Never ever forget, you earn everything you get. Once you embrace yourself, and love yourself, the sky's the limit.

Exercise

Practice this every morning: wake up and be aware of how everything in your body is working. You're breathing, your heart is beating, your eyes can open, you can smell, hear, feel, taste. Be grateful for that. Get out of bed and walk. Think of people who don't have legs. Those with missing hands. Then look at your fingers. Think about what your fingers accomplish for you on a daily basis. Recognize how alive you are and feel grateful for this gift.

Walk around the house, apartment, or wherever you live, and admire the fact that you have a roof over your head. You have a bed. You have a toilet. You have a kitchen. Your mission in this is to wake up and feel gratitude. Practice this every day and I bet in time you will notice a change in your personality. When your perspective changes for the better, then you change for the better.

Chapter 8

Choices

When you're faced with the ultimate decision—life or death—what do you choose? Obviously, I chose to do drugs—and that was a choice to step away from life. I take full responsibility for those choices. I chose to do drugs and all that came with it.

Then I chose to give sobriety a chance. I chose to believe rehab might just work. I chose to listen and truly hear the instructions at the facility. I chose, after the first three months in rehab, to accept the fact that I can never drink again. I chose to live a daily life devoted to thinking and acting upon my sobriety.

Daily decisions are based on our choices. So much of my life was taking chances. I had good outcomes and bad ones. That's life, right? I don't want to regret not taking chances. When I was faced with challenges that I believed I could achieve, I did them. I also did them when I didn't believe in myself. I just wanted to know that I was willing to try.

As a child I was always willing to be bold, and a lot of times suffered a negative consequence. Something that I found very effective in sobriety was being able to think back and recognize things that happened in my life that played a huge role in my decision-making.

When I was about ten, my brother, myself, and the neighborhood kids decided to have a water gun fight—no, better to call it a war. We had it out in the forest. There were teams, perimeters, and once you got shot, you had to play dead until one man stood victorious. This kind of game was a blast. With movies like Rambo back in the 80's, we thought we were all real live Green Berets. So, the game began, and I shot a couple of players and felt that my moment was coming. As I noticed one of my teammates down, I asked him who "killed" him. He replied, "It was Rob. He's the last guy on his team, and you're the last guy on our team." Rob, my older brother. My nemesis. My arch-rival who had beaten me at everything since I was born. My entire life I had lost to this villain. This might just be the moment I could finally beat my older brother at something.

With my vast knowledge of the woods, I had a very good idea of where my brother was hiding. At that point though, I had a dilemma. I had to take a shit really, really, badly. The house was a quarter mile away. I could run home, shit, then go shoot my brother and earn my rightful crown as the neighborhood sharpshooter. Or, I could go shoot Rob, then go home and take a victory shit. Oh no, I want to bathe in the moment of victory, so I chose home first.

I ran home dodging trees, doing spin moves, jumping over rocks and moving like a gazelle. As I approached a tree that had fallen down years before, I made the assumption that I could jump this with no issues. I was sadly mistaken in my calculations of my athleticism and I tripped face-first into the forest floor. My chest broke most of the impact, and I saw a cloud of dust puff as my face met the dirt. As I got to my feet, I tasted dirt in my mouth, and saw stars… and then an unfortunate warm sensation in the back of my pants. I had shit myself.

I walked home delicately. Once I arrived home, I said hello to my mother, who was in the living room. Relieved she was nowhere near the washing machine, I threw my shitty underwear in it, wiped my ass somewhat, got a new pair of undies on, and went back into the wilderness.

I was back in the game. It was the moment of victory I had been waiting for, and I knew exactly where my brother was—he was hiding under his favorite rock. I approached his location with imaginary ninja-like skills. I reached the top of the boulder and made my move. With skills Rambo would have envied, I shot my brother with laser-like precision.

I was the absolute winner—ruler of the forest! I had done it! I had beaten my brother. I had earned the respect of the neighborhood kids. I saw the mission through—despite some personal discomfort— and accomplished it. Oh, how sweet that victory would be for years to come!

As I was jumping up and down with excitement, instead of lying down "dead," my brother came out from under the rock and attacked me, giving me a bloody nose. I ran home to tell my mom, but before I could tell her, she smacked me right across the face. "You put a huge poop in the laundry machine! Does that make sense to you? You're grounded. Go to your room."

I was crying so hard I couldn't breathe. I went to my room and couldn't believe what just happened. I worked so hard to achieve to beat my brother Rob at something—and this was my reward? I had done what I had to do to win. I made a choice, and I wasn't ashamed of it. To make matters worse, my ass itched like crazy because I didn't wipe my ass correctly.

At times we make choices. Sometimes, with those choices, we're presented with other problems. We have to deal with the consequences of those choices. Kids make bad choices all the time. Adults teach kids on how to best deal with those situations and make sure they learn from those mistakes. The choices that I made in the forest that day had an impact on me. It made me want to rebel against making good decisions. Most kids feel that way at some point in their life. Most kids learn from it, get over it, and move on. I learned from a lot of mistakes over the years, got over them, and moved on. At some point, my frustration with my bad choices started to get the best of me. Where is it that I lost sight of learning from it, getting over it, and moving on from it? These were questions that needed to be answered in rehab.

Sometimes my willingness to take chances hurt me. I don't love learning things the hard way, but I sure am consistent at it. I just happen to be one of those people who makes a choice, then regrets it later. Even in my years of recovery, I had the courage to make the difficult decisions, then suffered the consequence. That's what makes choices fascinating, though. When I speak of regretting it later, I'm not talking about events that hurt me or my sobriety— but I was often embarrassed. I say and do things very impulsively. When I see people reacting negatively, I can't help but think, "Dammit! I did it again."

When I look back at the choices I made during addiction, I can't help but realize I was consistently making bad ones. That's just the truth of addiction decision-making. If I was making good decisions, it was only good for my selfishness. During rehab, I noticed a shift in my decision-making. I didn't feel in control of my choices when I was under the influence. Rehab provided time and logic to heal my thought process. Once I felt that I was back in control, I was then able to analyze each choice I made. I remember feeling extremely frustrated with the facility because I was just frustrated in general. I wasn't being held against my will. I wasn't legally bound there. If I wanted to leave the facility, I could have. But, I didn't. I made a choice in rehab, even in my frustration, that I would give the program a chance. Maybe I would complete the program, then go out and use again, but I wanted to give rehab a real chance. I would give it my all.

In recovery, choices are hard, especially in the first year. It's a whole new world when you sober up. Choices and decision-making are a daily challenge. But in time, it gets better, and easier. When you consistently make the right choices, even when you don't want to, you find that life starts to become easier.

Look at your thought process as a house. It's your house. It's your temple. You're the cleaning lady, the maintenance man, and the landscaper. Do you have a house of horror, or is it your dream house? The choice is yours. When you are an addict, you forget to keep your house clean. You wake up one day and wonder why you live in such a shitty neighborhood. Why is the house—your thoughts— a house of horror? Once you get fed up with your current condition, what's next? Do you clean your own house, or do you try to pay someone to clean it? Even if you go to rehab, at some point, you discover the truth. If you want something done right, you need to do it yourself. That is where the healing begins. That is where your greatest choice is felt. The choice you've decided to make is sobriety.

Over the years I've watched my behavior toward my cell phone evolve. I made an effort to allow myself only limited time on my cell each day. I was also mindful of what my purpose was for being on the device—was I just wasting time, or did I need it to accomplish something? I researched the power of persuasion used in these cell phone apps, and why they feel addictive. I love my cell phone and always have. Not only was I addicted to drugs, but I over-consumed my cell phone as well. Obviously, I need to be careful with anything addictive. These choices made a huge difference in my day. I started to become more focused on the things I truly valued. I felt more productive with my days. A cell phone can either be like an addictive drug, or it can be like a vitamin for your mind. If used inappropriately, you can become dependent on it and eventually it will cause harm to your day. If used wisely, it can become a tool to help educate you and help you grow with each day.

Here's another choice I made: I noticed that when I was watching television, and daydreaming about irritating aspects of my day, I would change the channel. Numerous times I thought to myself, "Why'd you just change the channel? I was watching that." What I discovered was that *I was trying to change my thoughts*. I didn't like thinking about irritating things that I couldn't change. I felt like I had no control in my head, so I tried to control what I could—the television channel. I laughed at myself when I recognized what I was doing, but it got me thinking. Every time I have over-consuming negative thoughts, I need to say, "change the channel." I started doing this every day, and noticed that most of the time it worked. When it didn't work, it just required a little more focus on finding something productive to think about. Truth is, I got tired of my thoughts dictating how I felt for the next few hours. I made a choice to fight those thoughts by changing them. By making that choice I was able to see a problem, find a healthy solution, and practice that solution with humor.

Recognize how your choices affect your emotions. Feel the difference. When you feel that difference, you know you've made a healthy choice.

Some of the smallest choices we make can be among the most impactful. Some happen within a blink of an eye. The window between an action and a reaction is so brief that it seems like it's more of an impulsive decision. Here's an example: Someone makes an antagonistic comment to you. That's the moment. That's the very brief window where they performed the action, and they now wait in anticipation for your reaction. What's your state of mind looking like at the time? If you've been having a bad day, then it's more likely that your reaction will not be good. If you're in a great mood and feeling well, then you're more likely to react in a positive manner. How many times in your life have you made an impulsive decision in that scenario? How many times have you made a well-thought-out decision in that situation? The question now becomes, what can you do to strengthen your character in that window?

We spent years in our addiction consistently

making impulsive decisions. We spent zero time negotiating with ourselves about going and getting our drugs. No time to think, just go get it. Within our sobriety and recovery, we start to understand the importance of thinking before reacting. We begin to understand that the choices we make in each moment can dictate our success in recovery.

Anger and frustrations can lead you to make some bad choices. Anger is absolutely a part of being a human being. Don't allow anger to make the choice for you. When we allow anger to get the best of us, we're more likely to relapse.

When we practice being at peace with ourselves, confident with ourselves, and hold ourselves to higher standards, we never allow a stranger to get under our skin. Now that sounds wonderful, but that can be very challenging when in recovery. I felt very vulnerable and sensitive in my recovery. Other times, I felt very confident and peaceful. When I practice making good choices all day, every day, that's when I feel more confident. By making good choices all day long I'm reminding myself that this is the new me, and I'm letting go of the old me.

In sobriety, and throughout life, you're going to feel negative emotions. It's a part of the human experience. Allowing those thoughts to expand out of control is where you allowed your poor choices to bring you down. That's no one else's fault. You did it.

I think a lot about my years as an addict and all the poor behaviors that come with that. I was a bullshitter, manipulator, and a liar. Ultimately, I was lying to myself. With sobriety, I'm able to practice these daily thoughts, behaviors, and choices for a life of sobriety. The more I practice it—which is every moment of every day—the more I find sobriety to be a success as an adult, as a husband, as a son. Sobriety is a mentor. Sobriety is a guru. Sobriety makes me want to grow into a better man.

You're going to feel fear, frustration, and irritation in sobriety. Those are normal emotions that we all deal with. What I'm trying to present is the opportunity to recognize what's bothering you, and deal with it. Because if you don't, your mind will take you down a road of fear, frustration, and irritation for minutes, hours, and possibly days to come. With that comes the possibility of relapse. So, these choices that you make every day, matter. I choose to channel my addictive thoughts for an energy that creates positive results, not destructive ones. That's the choice I make every single moment, of every single day. Every single choice you make effects how sobriety will go for you. When you take responsibility for choices, sobriety becomes beautiful. When faced with the ultimate decision, I chose life!

Exercise

Consider this: every single move you make, every choice you make—you own that. Take full responsibility for the outcome. Even when you know you didn't do anything wrong, when the outcome is negative, take responsibility for it anyway.

Write down five choices you made recently. Really look at them. Could you have made a different choice? When you make a bad choice, that's all right, write it down. Then write down what you could've done differently. The point of the exercise is to learn from your choices whether good or bad. We make choices all day, every day. What we want to get better at is making the right choices even when we don't want to. Relapse is just waiting for us to make a couple of bad choices. When you write these things down and consciously think about them, you're more likely to make good choices.

Chapter 9

Better vs. Bitter

When you deal with adversity, does it make you better or bitter? Do you allow tough situations to strengthen your character, or eat at your pride and make you angry?

When I lived in the South, I had just finished college and was no longer playing football—which meant I wasn't working out anymore. I ate a lot of fast food and BBQ—the South has some bomb-ass BBQ that makes you want to slap yo momma! I also drank every single night. Naturally I gained weight. Co-workers would crack jokes at me in good fun. I'd play it off, but inside, it offended me. In my mind, I still thought I was in good shape. Instead of recognizing that I was behaving in an unhealthy way, I would drink to drown out my co-workers "busting my chops." This led to me becoming bitter.

As a man in recovery, it's important for me to recognize those situations where I'm feeling bitter and need to replace those emotions with better. In rehab, I had the opportunity to address my problems. Bitterness, on a grand scale, was at the root of my addiction. Playing out those scenarios in my head, and formulating a plan to address them, was hard work, and required that I battled these bitter feelings constantly.

My addiction stemmed from an internal bitterness. I made the choice to take one pain pill a month; then a week, then a day. That's the process. We make excuses for our actions. Those actions originated in a place called bitterness, because bitterness is easier to achieve. Our objective is to minimize the bitterness.

If you make an effort every single moment of every single day, then you're more likely to minimize bitterness. But it takes practice. Every day I have thoughts of bitterness. The best way to combat that bitterness is by being better. Sounds easy, but it's far from that. When you face bitterness and recognize it as nothing more than an immature emotion, then you're on the right track. I look at bitterness as similar to a dream. I wake up from a dream and feel confused as to why that crazy shit popped into my head. I try to make sense of it, but it never does. Best thing to do is let it go. Looking at bitterness as an immature thought, or a pointless dream, helps you practice being better.

Negative thoughts only hurt us in the end, because they only create a bitter state. How do we get better in this scenario? I'm an addict, which means I love the art of manipulation. Is there a way I can have a positive effect on this negative individual at work? My first thought is to lead by example. Positivity will always prevail, just do it right. So, you lead by example, you're friendly to this person even in the face of their demon-like demeanor. You treat them the same way you treat everyone in the office and still, they're an evil ass bitch. Shit! All right, we've got to step our game up. Now you want to get to know their interests, their lifestyle: what they eat, drink, do they exercise? The whole shot. We then start giving them hints toward a different way of looking at things. Say you saw a video on someone who did this, and it seemed to work. You go through all of this, just to try your very best at getting this person to be less evil. At some point you realize, that didn't work either.

The only person you can truly control is you yourself. The power of positivity needs to be felt, especially by a person in recovery. You can't waste your time allowing another person's misery to make you miserable. How many times in your recovery have you been courteous to others, only to receive a lack of courtesy in return? Those scenarios are exactly where we can become bitter. This world is filled with bitterness and selfishness. That doesn't mean you need to join that club. In fact, in your sobriety you can't afford to join that bitter bunch. When you practice being courteous and expect people to be the same in return, you will be disappointed. When you practice being courteous, and have no expectations in return, that's when you'll feel the shift. When you have expectations of other people's behavior you will see both a good outcome, and a bad one. Be at peace with both. In my experience, the toughest part of practicing being better is when I'm surrounded by bitter individuals spewing their negativity. By working on being better and being at peace with who I am, and what I represent, I'm keeping my integrity in check. If you practice being better every time you encounter negativity, then you are in fact practicing a better you. This is one of the tougher aspects of sobriety.

Grateful vs. Greedy

One of the major issues in our world is greed; it's at the root of so many of the world's issues. Sobriety forces you to be grateful for this second chance. If you make the effort to see yourself as grateful instead of greedy, then you will start to become hypersensitive to greedy behaviors. That sensitivity helps you identify the behavior, then quickly stop it. Greed can often be explained by a person being unsatisfied about something in their life. As addicts, greed is beautiful. As a sober man, greed is counterproductive to the goal at hand.

When I used drugs, the last thing on Earth I wanted to do was share. Being consistently high was what I set out for. There's no sharing in that scenario—at least for me there wasn't. On top of that, I was never satisfied. I wanted more and more. We've all seen or heard of stories where money made someone so greedy that it ruined them, their career, and then their family. It was money that made them travel down that road.

Drug addicts go through the same thing every day. The high is the same thing as the money. There's just never enough of it. It's the thrill of the chase and that greediness is where it all comes crashing down. Most people love achieving goals, and chasing that high provides that goal-achieving feeling. Obviously, the drugs get you high, but so does the thrill of the chase, seek and destroy, or accomplishing goals. You feel a sense of success. Where is it that we become greedy? When we act for the sake of self-centeredness, rather than the betterment of others. Greed is when peace of mind gets manipulated into believing that *more* equals happiness. What more equals is addiction. Greed eventually comes crashing down, and what's left after that is the recognition of what you once had. Of course, that all depends on if you live to tell the tale.

When you pursue your recovery with gratitude, you learn a lot about yourself. After going through the experience of addiction and feeling greed, you find yourself grateful for the basic things that life has to offer—that is, life itself, family and friends, a place to live, transportation, food, and a love for yourself. Most people can admit to neglecting a level of gratitude for those things at times. After years of addiction and greed, it's the little things that provide so much hope and happiness. When you achieve things like the job you desired, or the clothing you worked hard to save for, or getting your body in shape, you feel a sense of achievement. You feel grateful because you *earned* it, and truly worked hard to achieve it without greed. Even in our life of recovery we enjoy the thrill of the chase. You chase down every little thing you need to do to achieve each goal, like the job you wanted. In pursuit of getting your body in the shape you want you need to seek and destroy each workout. What makes being grateful different from greedy is when you respect and love the rough road you traveled for success, versus doing everything you can to find a short cut.

Hero vs. Villain

Let's talk about the hero—the better—and the villain—the bitter. We all want to be heroes. Few people set out to be the villain of their own personal story. People give in to drugs or alcohol, and before they know it, they have become the villain of their nightmares. It's the hero, and only the hero, who can defeat the villain.

That hero is within you every single moment of every single day. Bring him out!

There are a lot of characteristics that describe a hero: self-confidence, responsibility, courage, honesty, hard-working, being driven, having focus, and that's just to name a few. Being your own hero starts when you decide to give sobriety a chance. That takes an abundance of courage to face your addiction demons. The hero within is the one who will stand strong against the voice of the villain that will continuously tempt you to use again.

The characteristics of the villain consist of being irresponsible, hateful, bitter, greedy, engaging in negative behavior, and that's just to name a few. The villain was exactly who we were during our addiction. We did everything the villain needed us to do to continue using drugs. It was the villain that provided us with the ideas on how to come up with the money to go get our drugs. It was the villain who made sure we knew just what to say so we could consistently get our way.

When we experience success, love, progress, peace of mind, even a good exercise workout, it triggers a chemical response in our brain that gives us a high. It's one of the hallmarks of hero behavior. Once you feel that high, then you continue to pursue it. We're addicts. It's what we do. When we work hard toward something, and feel that sense of achievement, we feel that high. When we behave in healthy ways, we become healthy—which is a natural high. This is what heroes do.

Our villain gets chemicals flowing in our brain as well. Think about moments you have when you see or hear drama, anger, or gossip; it can equal you feeling a high from that chaotic moment. Being an addict, aren't we going to consistently seek that high? That's what we do. That's the villain. When we watch the news, experience road rage, get angry at stupid stuff like grocery store selfishness, the line in the bank taking too long, etc., these all trigger that chemical response that gives us a high, even though we don't like the emotion. But somehow, we still chase that negative high every day. Why? Because we're addicts.

As addicts, it's important that we identify the difference between the hero and the villain. To find success in sobriety, we need to make better decisions versus bitter decisions. Today you woke up and your first thought was "Don't use drugs today." That's beautiful. That's what it takes.

I have been tested time and time again, and so will you. Recognizing the villains throughout the day allows you to be focused on your decision-making. The villain/bitter thoughts will be in your face every day. When you're able to identify those things as a choice, then you will find success. When you look at those things as non-negotiable, then you're making a conscious decision to be 100 percent invested into a healthier future.

One of the biggest problems we all face is how we feel internally—physically and mentally. The healthier we feel, the more likely we are to speak healthily. The more you feel internally gross, the more likely you are to speak grossly. When I feel shitty, I spew shitty comments towards others. I speak how I feel. Feeling internally ugly, gross, and shameful is the bitterness that I'm speaking about. Our bitterness eats and eats at us. We feel anger, we speak angrily.

How do we correct that feeling? By creating a lifestyle that minimizes the opportunity to feel ugly, gross, and shameful. Keep in mind that I said minimizing, not eliminating. No matter how healthy we eat, how much exercise we do, how often we meditate, it doesn't matter. Bad things happen and we either deal with it in a better way or bitter way. The choice is ours. Minimizing the emotions of bitterness is the objective.

Think of the habits that you've developed over the years. Your daily thoughts consist of some bitter shit, so it's going to take time to reprogram yourself. Even when you don't feel like being nice in public, force yourself to. Eliminate your selfishness and be good to others. Program your mind into believing that being good to others strengthens your character. Look outside yourself. When you don't try, you're allowing selfishness to take center stage. Be better to others and you will feel better about yourself. The more you practice this, the more you will feel a shift in your personality.

When an issue arises, and you find yourself becoming bitter, rewind the movie. You know when you're watching a movie and you need to back it up because you missed something important? That's how I treat my bitterness. I rewind the movie and play it back until the images in my head see a better result, not a bitter one. Practice making your personal movie one of positivity. What goes on in your head *is your responsibility*. Do not allow your thoughts to take you to bitter places. Be in control, and always remember that this takes moment by moment practice.

Exercise

Think about a moment in your life that caused you bitterness. Now imagine a positive outcome, or a way to look at it in a more positive, healthy way. Notice your feelings. Practice this every day until it becomes a habit. When you identify moments where you felt bitterness, then you recognize a chance to make changes. Bitterness consistently ends badly. So, when you imagine a better outcome, you're going to find it. This exercise is something you should practice mentally throughout the day.

Chapter 10

Values

Discovering what it was that I valued most was a key element to my sobriety. There were deeper lessons in my past, and I needed to understand them. What are my daily values? Having a strong character equals my self-esteem and not falling victim to addiction. Nothing is of value without struggle. Everything I value in life came from some sort of struggle. Whether small or big, struggle provided enlightenment.

I asked a variety of friends and family about their values. A friend told me she chased success for years, only to discover that peace was her actual objective. She values being able to have a calm state of mind, and a peaceful outlook on all that life throws her way.

I asked my stepdaughter, and she said having a good day is what she values. She described going to the park the other day. She took her dog, her son, and her grandmother for a birthday party that a friend was having. She said that the day couldn't have gone any better. Everyone was happy and having a good time: no family drama, no dysfunction, just pure fun. After all the years of growing up in poverty, she valued a good day. Good days were hard to come by in her upbringing.

"One day at a time," and the Twelve-Step Program present a beautiful theory. Having an addictive personality, however, I felt that philosophy wasn't going to work for me. For my impulsive decision-making, one day can feel like a lifetime. So much shit goes down in one day. So much shit can happen in less than a minute, especially in the mind of an addict. So instead, I believe every single moment, of every single day, matters. My emotions, like most people's, bounce around throughout the day. As an addict, I need to wake up in the morning and think of what I value most. Starting my day off with that in mind allows me to focus moment to moment.

Here's what I value: Integrity. I look at integrity as someone who does the right thing even when nobody's looking. I love integrity as a value because it's a personal analysis of oneself. It's you, holding yourself accountable. That's a huge part of addressing our addiction issues, taking responsibility for our actions. When we hold ourselves responsible for our own actions, that's what I mean by integrity.

Humility is another value I cherish. Most of us have a level of pride or stubbornness. I don't like to admit when I'm wrong, but I try to practice admitting when I am. I remember absolutely being right all the time when I was addicted to drugs. The only time I admitted defeat was when I was getting something out of the deal. Being humble helps the mind of an addict not over-think things. The greatest way to practice humility is by being honest with yourself. When you're honest with yourself, then you're honest with everyone else.

Communication is another great value. My ability to socialize with others was different in sobriety. For years I had some sort of substance in my body creating a false confidence. Socially, I had no trouble speaking when under the influence. In my years of sobriety, I've had to practice getting better at it. During our addiction, we spend so much time not caring about what other people think, so when we communicate, we have no discomfort. In our recovery, communicating with others helps us get back on track minus the drugs. It's all practice. I believe that listening to others is a huge benefit as well. In fact, listening can be even more important. I have found myself more observant in my years of sobriety. Listening shows the person you're communicating with that you care. It's the beauty of gathering information and showing that you retained it.

Friendship is another thing I value. I didn't understand this when I was an addict. As a drinker, I had a blast with fellow drunks, but eventually alcohol made me hate them. I decided I'd rather drink by myself than be around friends. When I added opiates on top of the booze, my attitude became "fuck friends, I have what I need," so I avoided them. I only wanted to be around people if they could get me what I wanted. When you're addicted to anything, there is only one important piece to every day: attaining your substance. Who gives a shit about friendship? The people I associated with to accomplish the daily goal were not friends—they were accomplices. The people I was getting my drugs from were in the same struggle as me. They had no values in their life, just like me. We had a common interest in drugs and that was all that mattered. And they were all I had.

Throughout rehab I heard a variety of people say, "Those people were not your friends. They don't care about you or your life. They're bad people." At first, I resisted that thought, because I felt just because we all did drugs didn't make them pieces of shit. As I achieved sobriety, I searched my soul and discovered I had a lot of associates and accomplices. The whole point of friendship is to feel the affection of togetherness—not use each other to get what we want. My true friends to this day are a small group. My friends care about me as a person and I feel the same about them. Our common interests aren't destructive. Our common interests are parallel.

The ugliest individual I encountered as an addict was myself. Looking in the mirror and seeing my face—transformed by years of chemical abuse into a death mask—was a horrific experience. I saw that me every day and hoped to die. Once I regained my self-esteem, identity, and love for life, I started to slowly love myself again. In time, with every day that passed, I loved what I was growing into in my new life of sobriety.

Even in sobriety, I find myself being judgmental toward others the way I was to that guy in the mirror. I see the ugliness. I see people bitter with one another, I see the comments on social media, and the anger on the highway with one another. I also see that I am all of that. I have those moments, too. When I'm judgmental of others, I always question if I feel that way because I see myself in them. That's hard to admit. Now when I do this, I find myself feeling really fucking ugly, because the answer is, yes. It's not an easy thing to do. It's not an easy practice. When you make this effort, you discover how much you should shut up, and be better than that! Your judgment of others dissipates because you're sick of seeing how ugly you, yourself, are.

Our greatest war is within. Once we come to terms with that, then the battle is already won. My greatest enemy within myself was met with compassion, not hate. I chose to understand him instead of attempting to destroy him. I can't kill off my addictive personality, only embrace him as a necessary equal who provides balance to my internal fight for a better life. Enemies are necessary to pit ourselves against, and achieve greatness. If the enemy is within, then we must learn to become teammates.

Sobriety forced me to reassess how I'd been doing things. I'd accepted the idea that selfishness was all right. That everything should come to me right away. Patience is for dummies. If I don't check those thoughts, then I become ugly, and that leads right back to using. Every single moment of every single day, an addict has decisions to make. Most people do not make an effort to better themselves. Addicts have no choice if they plan on staying sober.

As a teenager, my values were similar to a piece of lint floating through the air. You see it for a second, then it's gone. Once I hit high school, I played football and discovered ambition. As an athletic kid, I was very determined, passionate, and wanted to be the best. Football hit my emotions like heroin. I loved that first high of finding success with my teammates. My freshman year of high school, I had no doubt that I was going to go play college football.

My self-discipline while I played football was so strong that nothing distracted me. My self-destruction was so strong during my addiction that you couldn't convince me that I was going to live much longer. The difference between the two are, one's good, and one's bad. I love how similar they are though. Pure 100 percent focus on achieving a goal. I found it fascinating in rehab to reflect on my ability to go 100 percent in the things I was passionate about, even the bad things. With that thought, why can't I apply the same attitude to my sobriety? I was willing to destroy friendships, lie, steal, and cheat to get drugs, but I wasn't willing to do the opposite to enjoy a better life? Fuck that!

When I was released from rehab, I expected the world to be proud of me sobering up. I was met with disinterest. How could I fit in as a former addict into this crazy world? I wanted to tell the world about my story but recognized the judgment I would face. I wanted to explain myself, but recognized people didn't want to hear about it.

Going into the real world after rehab is a harsh experience, but so is addiction. I can't count how many times in my life I had the balls to just go for it—so why was sobriety any different? I know I'm no genius, but I'm a fucking maniac on a mission to prove addiction is beatable. The reason I felt that the world was so harsh when I first left rehab was a picture that I painted. It was within my own mind and own insecurities that I created this expectation. Once I recognized that, I was able to let go of the old me. I started to distance myself from some of the old insecurities. I told myself it was time to make the necessary changes.

When you say you're going to do something, hold yourself accountable. I know that's easier said than done. No one is going to hold your hand through any of this shit. Everything you do in life is your choice. You might have people who morally support you. You might have friends who cheer you on. But no one is going to do it for you. When you value something, choose integrity over comfort. Find your values and show that you live them.

On my third day out of rehab, I was wearing a pair of old cargo shorts that I hadn't seen since before rehab. I had just returned home from a job interview and was very enthusiastic about getting back into the world of work. I noticed a feeling like there was an old pack of gum in my pocket. When I returned home, I finally reached in my pocket to see what this annoyance was. I pulled it out, and discovered it was an old wrapped up piece of heroin that I had yet to smoke. This was a moment I had feared for the last six months. This was where I would find out whether rehab worked or not. You can try your best to avoid these situations, but the dirty-ass world of addiction will be in your face the remainder of your days.

As my brain attempted to process this situation, my instincts took over. My impulses jerked through my body quicker than my brain could process it. I raced to the bathroom and threw the heroin into the toilet. I flushed it and screamed, "Fuck you, bitch! I win, bitch!" I gave it the finger and yelled, "You'll never beat me again. I win, motherfucker! You ain't shit, bitch." I spat on the toilet bowl in anger, then went into my bedroom and laid on the bed to control my breathing.

After a minute or so, I was able to calm my thoughts and recognize what I had just achieved. This moment marked not only my greatest challenge, but my greatest fear. I had just looked heroin in the face and beat it for the first time. That was the win I needed. That was the win that allowed me to value my sobriety. I accepted, loved, and respected that my addiction would never leave me. That addiction voice in my head was me. I discovered that I valued that voice because *I love me.* That voice took me places beyond my worst nightmares. He's now shown me my potentiality as a man and what I can grow into. Because of him, I will be compassionate when faced with self-judgment. I will show desire for a better life when faced with self-pity. I will show determination when subjected to self-doubt. I will choose self-discipline before self-destruction. What I value more than anything in this world right now is my sobriety.

Exercise

Make a list of your top five values. That's sort of similar to asking you to write down your top five favorite rappers, singers, or athletes, right? I'm a Hip-Hop head, so let's talk rappers. One month, I might be all about Nas. Then the next month, I feel like Eminem is top dog. Then I go on a kick about Andre 3000. Your values will change at times. That's all right. That's part of the process. These values need to be seen and thought of on a daily basis. When you see them, or think about them, then you're more likely to practice those values throughout your day.

Chapter 11

Robot Behaviors

I'm frightened of the day we're surrounded by robots. Technology is advancing, and it's likely we will get to a point where we have robots in our homes completing a variety of tasks for us. I worry that humans will lose our ability to be resourceful, and we'll lose our sense of purpose. Can you imagine how lazy we would all become? I don't like folding clothes, but it gives me a sense of pride and responsibility. The more I have a robot taking care of my responsibilities, then what use am I? I'm concerned that robots will take our jobs. What use are we when robots do everything?

As concerned as I am about our future robot overlords, I'm frightened of my own robotic behaviors. We are all creatures of habit. We use muscle memory at some point every day. The consistency of being repetitive with our same routines every day is similar to having a robot do these things for us. What happens is, we get so used to the routine that we forget to enjoy our lives. Day in and day out, we continue these repetitive acts with no thought. We have our routines, daily rituals, consistent habits that we all do. We're programmed to go with the flow. We do those things in a robotic way. I'm not saying that's bad. I follow a routine, too. But to get and stay sober we have to evaluate which robotic behaviors are helping us, and which are hurting us.

Any routine you have going right now, question. Are you just going through the motions? Is this what you really want to be doing? Is there something else you need to do for your current situation? Analyze if you should be doing more. Are you stuck in your routine and not growing, not looking to be better? Robot behaviors happen to all of us. Too often we look back years later and wonder what the fuck we did with those years? When I was in rehab, I absolutely thought about the last six years, and my addiction to opiates. On top of that, what was I doing as a drinker for thirteen years? Those years are gone. Think about what you want to do differently in this next chapter of your life.

When you take your sobriety seriously, you start a whole new life. During addiction, you had some internal emotional issues that were not being dealt with. Once you started to identify what those issues were, the objective was to address them, letting go of the old you. In many respects, all of us who have been through addiction just want a restart. We just want to let go of the old baggage. Recovery gives you the perfect opportunity to start a whole new you. Now when you start this new you, what behaviors do you want to consistently practice every day—that will benefit your recovery—versus getting sucked into robotic behaviors that can lead to a possible relapse?

Throughout this book, I've been giving suggestions as to what helps us have success in each day. Those types of repetitive actions are healthy. You want to practice being thoughtful about every move you make. That's what helps us achieve this whole new us. Now, when we end up doing the same things over and over every day—with no intent behind our thought processes—that's when things get dangerous. I practice certain repetitive thoughts every day. Here's an example: "I'm an optimistic person. I love that I'm optimistic. I think about my optimism often. I love a pessimist because they remind me of who I am, an optimist. I believe that if I was to throw a pile of shit in the air, that it would come back down to earth as gold. Why? Because I'm optimistic."

With that thought, I believe what I'm doing is meaningful for my recovery. I deal with a level of anxiety often, and here and there a little depression, but I embrace those emotions as a necessary means to a positive end. I don't want to paint this picture that everything in my life is wonderful. Recovery is hard. In recovery we are going to be hypersensitive to emotions. We've been numbing the pain for years. By practicing my thoughts of optimism, I'm trying to be robotic for the *right reasons*. I absolutely want to change the game on the statistics of relapsing by being robotic and repetitive with conscious thought about optimism, even when it feels like my life sucks. I'm maximizing my openness to be this whole new me. Robotic behaviors that consist of conscious thought and have good intent are exactly what we should desire.

Let's evaluate some of the robotic behaviors that are hurtful to our progress. Start with the smaller details of your day. Evaluate your workout routine or any consistent physical activity that you find yourself bored with. When we go through the motions at the gym, we end up losing interest. What drinks are you mindlessly chugging down—coffee, soda, energy drinks? What kind of snacks do you reach for thoughtlessly? I'm not trying to be offensive, please know that I have mindlessly and thoughtlessly over-consumed sugar drinks and unhealthy snacks in my years of recovery. In the chapter about Self-Care, we'll talk about a healthier lifestyle and eating pattern. A lot of our decision-making with drinks and foods are robotic behaviors.

Some of the bigger issues can be finances, work, and leisure time. Addicts have a tendency to just go for it and suffer the consequences later. Making more of an effort toward how you spend your money helps your financial situation. If you are consistently making purchases that add up to a lot of money, that can be hurtful to your situation in your recovery.

Work can be a very repetitive process every day. I find myself being robotic at work often. What helps me the most in those situations is present-time thinking. I try to focus on being the best at my job with each given task. Work can also be challenging as we deal with a variety of issues—like an unpleasant boss, co-worker, or the job itself. We sometimes find that by being robotic, we keep ourselves safe from those challenges.

My robotic behaviors in certain jobs have been to make sure I do the job correctly, but I often don't want to have to interact with certain people at work. I just want to do my job and get back to my personal life. So, what happens is, I end up getting too robotic with my routines at work. But this behavior can make me look like an asshole because I'm not interested in socializing with others. In recovery, it's very beneficial to practice social skills. We're social beings, we're supposed to be socializing. So, my robotic behavior at work was not beneficial. My way of counteracting this behavior was by attempting to change my routine by socializing more frequently. It takes effort on my part, but the more I branch out and distance myself from my robotic behaviors, then the more I learn about others.

Leisure time can be very robotic if you're not paying attention. You need to unwind and enjoy life, but if you are doing the same activity over and over, it will lose its excitement at some point. Keep things fresh—change things up from time to time to make your leisure time more interesting.

Robot behaviors can lead to self-destruction, misery, complacency, and possible depression.

When you are not consciously thinking about your actions, you can easily slide down that hill of drug use again.

Exercise

Analyze one whole week of your behavior: the days you work, and the days you are off. Where is it in those days that you have small, or even large robotic behaviors? Write them down. Acknowledge the existence of those behaviors. Identify where they are, and how you can improve them if need be. Also, in this analysis, acknowledge the healthy robotic behaviors you have. The big objective here is not to lose sight of your identity.

Chapter 12

The Effect of a Butterfly

In life, we have moments that impact us for short periods of time; others affect us forever. There are also moments that impact us, fade away, then come back later in life to remind us what truly matters most. At the age of eleven, I witnessed my fourteen-year-old brother break his neck snowboarding on a skateboard with no wheels. That moment had repercussions that affected my life in ways I never anticipated.

Growing up in the Sierra Nevada Mountains, our backyard was wilderness: mountains, trees, rocks, hills, trails, wildlife, etc. The day of the accident was a typical winter day, with snow on the ground and overcast skies. Four of the neighborhood kids were out. All of us were suited up in our winter coats, pants, boots, and gloves. The big thing back then was who was going to be the first to accomplish a new goal. We found a big rock that had a cliff off of it. It was angled so you could stand on it, get on your board, slide down the rock about four feet, then slide off its edge—and then you were faced with the challenge of landing on a steep slope with trees and bushes all around. Landing was tricky, because our feet were not strapped in. The rock jump represented another opportunity for any of us in the neighborhood to do this stunt before my brother Rob did. He was generally the one to accomplish these challenges before us. Nothing would taste sweeter than getting this before him!

The neighborhood kids and I went out there before my brother made his way out. As I was about to go down the rock, I noticed Rob in the distance. It was now or never! I jumped on the board and went down the rock, jumped off, and miraculously landed with both feet on the board. I had achieved the impossible!

I looked back at my brother. Rob was staring at me with that competitive drive in his eyes. Shouting, "I can do that shit," he got up on the rock and started to slide down. Suddenly, the board slipped off to the right, but his momentum continued downhill. He fell off the board, plummeting forward. His head snapped back with a violent crack as he hit the ground, and his body slid down the hill a couple more feet.

We were all stunned.

Rob looked at me with the worry of life or death in his face and screamed, "I'm paralyzed! I'm paralyzed!" My brother could not feel anything from the waist up. His arms were useless to get him off the ground. He told me to come help him up. I didn't understand at that time the danger of me attempting to help him. I should have left him lying down and staying still until we could get an ambulance. I struggled to get my brother upright—he was a solid block of muscle after his freshman year of football. Somehow, I pulled him to his feet, and we slowly got up the hill to our neighbor's house because my parents were out shopping for Christmas. The neighbors immediately took Rob to the hospital.

For the next three months, my brother was in the hospital with screws in his head which were connected to the wall to keep his head in place. Once he left the hospital, he had to wear a halo, which was a very strange-looking contraption. There was something that looked like a sleeveless vest wrapping his upper torso in armor. It had metal rods connected from the chest and back sticking up toward the head, then those rods are connected to a metal rod wrapped around the head area. That metal halo was connected to rods that are drilled into the skull. His days of being a competitive athlete were gone. The doctors advised him never to play contact sports again. This was devastating for him. In the world of high school, athletes were kings. When Rob was no longer allowed to play sports, his friends disappeared on him. This one moment changed his life forever.

This moment changed my life as well. My brother was my hero and still is. What crushed me was that he set the standard in which I viewed competitiveness. With him no longer being allowed to play contact sports, he lost that aspect of his identity. This led me to find my own identity in the world of competitiveness. At the time I didn't understand the magnitude of this moment. Somehow, I felt as if I needed to compete for both of us.

When I was in rehab, it was a part of the program to identify where it was that I remember showing addictive personality traits. My brother's unfortunate accident is what led to me having an obsessive approach to athletics.

As I entered my eighth-grade year, my brother was in his senior year, but was not, of course, able to return to sports. The varsity football team was doing well that year and I started to notice a change in my brother. He'd rough me up, throwing me to the ground, and smack my face up a little bit.

He was particularly violent regarding a guy we'll call Frank (for the sake of avoiding legal ramifications). Rob would hit me and yell, "Don't you ever be like Frank!" who was the star running back on the varsity football team. All I could think was, "Who the hell is Frank?" My brother wanted to make sure I would never be as cocky as Frank, who was apparently very into himself.

In my crew of friends was a kid named Fella. He had an outgoing personality, was funny, and had the greatest laugh I've ever heard. Fella and I talked a lot about sports—it was our true passion. Fella excelled at baseball, and I loved football. There were numerous days I would come to school upset because my brother had beaten me the day before—Fella was the only one I told. The next school year, Fella went to the high school on the other side of town that had a better baseball program.

I had just finished up my freshman year of football and was at a high school party—the senior class were cool to me and would often invite me to their parties. As I was walking through this house, I spotted Frank—the man, the myth, the cocky running back who inspired brotherly beat-downs for me. Two females were draped over each of his shoulders. But what the fuck was this college guy doing at a high school party?

Frank called my name out with a stern look in his eye, as if he had really important Mafia business to talk to me about. He said, "I heard you had a good year. Not as good as me. You won't beat my rushing record. You're not as good as me." He yapped some more about some shit that I don't remember because I was still dumbfounded by the stupidity that he'd just spat in my face.

Right then and there, I changed my whole way of looking at this football thing. I stopped drinking, smoking herb, and focused on getting in the best shape possible to beat Frank's record. My sophomore year, I made the varsity team. Football season went well, and I was on track to beating Frank's record, or that was the plan.

I met up with Fella on New Year's Eve. We partied, and had a blast seeing one another. A week later, Fella was tragically killed over a *ten-dollar bet*. A man took a shotgun and blew a hole in Fella's chest. I was devastated. Death is one thing when it's your grandparents, but when it's a friend in your age group, it's different.

I became close friends with his family and had frequent visits with his mom, Verna. In my attempt to help Verna through her grief, I was also being helped by her. It was nice to develop a friendship with her and her family about this tragic situation.

I continued my quest to beat Frank's record; he'd played in twelve games and rushed for 1,089 yards his senior year.

My senior year, on the fifth game of the season, I was 59 yards away from beating Frank's record. My teammates were well aware of my goal; they wanted it too. This was a team thing. The story of my quest to beat the record became a big deal around town. I loved that Verna, my parents, and my hometown were present to see us as a team accomplish this goal.

Verna was hiding out at the top of the stadium away from the bleachers. She was one of those fans who preferred to be by herself when watching these games. The local sports reporter recognized her because of Fella's success in baseball and the coverage of his passing. He asked her what brought her to the game. She said, "I'm here to see Dave Atherton beat that asshole's record."

As the two were talking, there was an announcement that I was a few yards from breaking the record.

On the next play, I was handed the ball and made an eight-yard run. The loudspeakers proclaimed I had just beaten the record, surpassing Frank. My team-mates congratulated me, but I was so focused on the game that I didn't care. I couldn't process what I had just achieved. I remember smiling at my teammates and nodding my head. No words needed.

Hours after the game, I went to Verna's house. She smiled, laughed, and cried tears of joy with me for accomplishing this goal. Then she said she really needed to tell me something. She said that while she was talking to the reporter, a white butterfly was flying around her face and head. In fact, the butter-fly was being so persistent, she started laughing and told the reporter, "I don't mean to sound weird, but when something like this happens, I swear it's my son saying hello to me." They continued talking and the butterfly flew off.

They watched my next run and heard the big announcement. She was jumping, screaming, cry-ing, laughing, and felt extreme excitement for me. When she looked down at me in the huddle, she saw a white butterfly land on my helmet.

As she told me this, I started to cry. My body got warm and I felt true peace. There was a bit of shock mixed with this serenity and joy. We both cried and laughed, knowing that this story would have an im-pact on both of us for life.

My perspective on life changed in that single conversation. I worked my ass off to accomplish a goal. My drive stemmed from an arrogant teenager talking shit to me. I wanted to honor my dead friend by continuing to work hard at sports versus seeking vengeance. I wanted to make my brother proud because he was always my idol. I wanted to accomplish this goal and prove to myself I could do this. The record itself was accomplished, but the fact that my dead friend's mother was able to smile, laugh, and cry tears of joy for the first time in years was the true accomplishment. My hard work paid off in ways that I never imagined.

I also discovered that Frank was nothing but a nineteen-year-old talking shit. He was a kid himself. I was not mad at him. In fact, I can't thank him enough because he sparked an anger inside of me that pushed me to new levels of achievement. I was never mad at my brother for the beat-downs, I just wanted to make him proud of me, since he was unable to play sports.

In life we set goals: some take extremely hard work. When you sweat, when you bleed, when you cry, all for the sake of believing in achieving a goal, you learn so much more. I set out to beat a high school rushing record and ended up honoring my friend and helping his grieving mother.

This story is a reminder of how certain moments have a huge impact on our lives. This moment helped trigger an avalanche of happiness. Not only did it help Verna, but it helped all of Verna's family and friends. My brother and I absolutely love and respect one another these days.

So how is it that I became an alcoholic and drug addict years later? Having an addictive personality is a unique situation to be in. My obsession to achieve a goal, especially something I like, is undeniable. The adrenaline rush I got from that moment during the game was something I wanted to experience again. Heroin addicts will often talk about the first time they tried the drug, felt its effects, then chased that same feeling for the remainder of their addiction. I loved football, and I loved helping create happiness for others. What I failed to realize was how to channel these emotions appropriately. As the years passed after my on-field success, I continued to conquer goals in the sport of football. Once football was done, then the only feeling that got close to the adrenaline rush of football was alcohol and any other drugs I could get my hands on.

When we look back on lessons we once learned, then forgot, we can feel depressed. Let's say your mom taught you a valuable lesson when you were young, then years later you became an addict. Once you sober up, you look back on that moment, and you're embarrassed. It hurts your ego to look back at lessons learned and acknowledge that you knew better than that. That happens often in sobriety. It's hard to admit that you knew better, but you still abused drugs and alcohol anyway. Why? The answer is simple, it's because you're an addict. In our moments of addiction, we didn't know how to channel that energy.

The Effect of a Butterfly

Exercise

In this exercise, write down some of the lessons and impactful moments you've learned in life, that you ended up losing sight of. Once you write those down, really think about them. Think about how impactful they can now be in your life of sobriety. Please note that you didn't do anything wrong by losing sight of these lessons. You were destined to become an addict. You needed to go through addiction to appreciate this current moment in your life. By writing these moments down it allows you to re-connect with that once impactful moment. How can that moment now affect you in your future of sobriety?

In loving memory of Alfonso "Fella" Mejia
1978-1994

Chapter 13

Insecurities and Vulnerabilities

The more we value things outside of our control, the less control we have. ~ Epictetus

Insecurities are what led to my addiction. We all have insecurities, but the question becomes, how do we deal with them? Being vulnerable is one of your greatest--but most rewarding--challenges in sobriety, and in life.

When I was ten years old, I had to get stitches in my dick because of a bike accident. My bike didn't have grips on the handlebars so when I crashed it was metal on flesh. I was staying at my best friend's house, so when this happened, his mom took me to the emergency room. She called my Dad--who was at work. When my Dad walked in to see how I was doing he observed that the doctor was stitching up my little innocent shaft. I saw my Dad fall over like a tree, passing out. Years later I remember my Dad and my brother asking me if I got boners, and if so, which way did it point. Their reason for asking this was because the doctor told my Dad years before, that he wasn't sure which direction my dick would point because the scar tissue would affect my erections. I said, "It goes to the left. I figured since I'm left-handed, and left-footed, why wouldn't my dick curve to the left?"

Throughout the years, I had insecurities about my dick because I was sure that everybody else had a normal dick, and mine was abnormal. I think it's hysterical now, but at the time it was devastating. I didn't talk to people about it. I was already frightened of having sex, because of STDs and pregnancy, but also because of my leaning dick. I wasn't sure if girls would like it or not. Once I reached a point of having sex, I noticed over the years that being drunk was almost a must. My insecurities ran so deep with the shape of my dick, I just figured I should be intoxicated, because at least then I won't really care whether they like it or not.

I refused to deal with those insecurities appropriately because it tested that typical teenage toughness. In my teens, I couldn't admit weakness or sensitivity. Guy's don't do that shit. At the time I didn't realize the ramifications of these insecurities, which can lead to some of our worst decision making. Eventually, that's what ended up happening. In my years of sobriety, I was lying in bed pondering on the last time, before I was with my wife, where I had sober sex. I was shocked to realize that the last time I was sober and had intercourse was when I was 20 years old. By feeling the necessity to be intoxicated I was more likely not to use protection. I was also more likely to make impulsive decisions. That's exactly what I did. I didn't care about the consequences until the next morning guilt kicked in. The best way to get rid of the next morning guilt was by getting intoxicated again. This dysfunctional cycle stemmed from my insecurities. This story is another example of things I needed to address when I was in rehab.

One of my insecurities when coming out of rehab was going out in public and talking to people. I doubted myself socially and convinced myself that people knew I was a former druggie. When I would interact with people in public, I would behave the way I told myself they saw me. Meaning, I believed they saw me as a druggie weirdo trying to be confident, when I wasn't. That's the way I would behave, because that's what I convinced myself they saw. Those deep insecurities that were happening within my head, were all me. I didn't know what anyone else was thinking, but I sure thought I did. I needed to change those thoughts and find a way to correct the anxiety.

My remedy for this was to make an effort to talk to people every day: store clerks, bank tellers, neighbors. No need for long drawn-out conversations; I started off small and just exchanged pleasantries. See if you can develop a real conversation. It wasn't easy for me. It took a lot of practice before I started to become comfortable doing this. Now it feels natural, and I'm less insecure about talking to strangers.

I've always been a people-pleaser, but what I've noticed is by doing that, I'm degrading myself. I found myself for years making an effort to get others to like me. That was absolutely a self-esteem thing. To this day, I want to be cool with others because I genuinely like people. But, because of that, I can easily lose sight of my authenticity. I'm not going out of my way to be a dick to anyone (because I'm a left-leaning dick which means I play it cool). I'm just not laughing at shit I don't find funny as much. I also don't like going along with a conversation that I don't agree with. Being a people-pleaser, I generally agreed with every conversation. I no longer go along with conversations, nor do I argue, I just simply listen.

During my years of sobriety, I wouldn't divulge any information about my addiction to co-workers. Firstly, it was private. Secondly, I felt it was socially awkward to spill those beans so quickly. Lastly, I feared their judgment. Because of those emotions I distanced myself from my co-workers. That distance between them made me bitter toward them. Since they couldn't relate to my issues, I had no use for them. Because of that attitude, I would end up working my brain into a frenzy during the work week, then unbelievably loving my days off. This attitude made me feel mentally sick.

I've learned to stop and evaluate these emotions. I'm sick for a week—I have a mental head cold. Those two days off always cured it. What does that tell me? If I was more honest about how I felt, maybe

I wouldn't feel sick. I disliked co-workers because of my own insecurities. I'm not honest about these feelings because I'm scared of being vulnerable with them. Because I work in the mental health field, I believe I'm supposed to have it all together. If I divulge that I'm a former addict, that'll show weakness. Showing weakness equals judgment.

I used to feel the same way out in public. I convinced myself that because of my addiction that people would view me as damaged goods. These insecurities made dealing with my sobriety very tough.

One of my worst insecurities is trying to be cool. I want to be perceived by others as a guy who knows what he's doing. When I fail at something, or make a mistake, I'm easily embarrassed. Why? I'm trying too hard to impress others instead of admitting to myself that I will never impress everyone. There's a huge weight on my shoulders when I try too hard at being cool. When I stop and try to understand what is happening, I come to the realization that trying to impress others gets you nowhere. Impress yourself. Allowing fear of acceptance from others to rule your decisions is self-defeating. A part of my issue with trying to be perceived as cool was because I've been guarded. When I allow myself to be vulnerable, or unguarded, I've found myself feeling free. Vulnerability allows me to break free, at least for that moment, and discover that I can get over this. What's crazy is, knowing this advice, and knowing I shouldn't care, but I still do. It takes practice. I have to keep trying.

Another insecurity I have is believing others are on a different level—and I tend to put some on a pedestal. When I sobered up, I was proud of myself, but still felt those insecurities about my behavior as an addict. That's where I put people on a pedestal and left myself beneath it. As an addict I hated myself and what I had become. That made me feel empty and "less than" other people. Gradually, I'm working on this insecurity. I may still put people on a pedestal, but now I'm learning I'm just as good as them. I can be an equal.

When a person agrees to go to rehab, there's a tiny, tiny bit of hope that it might work. They don't truly believe they will find the answers they seek, but they're willing to try. The addict has a willingness to go through pain and discomfort, conquer the insecurities about what life might be like without the crutch of a substance to lean on—that makes them beautifully vulnerable. In that moment, the addict is in unsafe, unguarded territory and they believe it's the right thing to do. In the times we force ourselves to be vulnerable, we find ourselves successful. Connecting the dots from insecure, to vulnerable, then to success, is what we want from the start. We must recognize being vulnerable as a part of the journey.

Fear is the most powerful insecurity. Fear is useful, because it keeps us alive: we're afraid of fire because we might get burnt; we're afraid of heights because we might fall, and so on. But fear is like addiction, taking control of your thoughts and actions.

I allowed fear to determine my decision-making. When I finally got over certain fears and found success in something, that voice still attempted to creep in and sabotage my progress. Once you get over a fear, bathe in that accomplishment. Don't let your thoughts and insecurities throw dirt in the tub.

Look at fear from the other point of view. Take the time to think about how many times you succeeded because you feared failure. That can be your driving force. When I found heroin in my pocket a week out of rehab, I was frightened of failing after six months in rehab. That fear drove me to make the right decision. I'm thankful for that because fear is very useful in that sense.

I look at fear as fighting fire with fire. Fear is a fire that can be used to destroy, or it can illuminate the darkness. Your resistance to fire ignites its power to destroy. To embrace the flame ignites its power to illuminate. The best way to fight fear is by using it to push you to success.

How many times have you made excuses not to go fulfill your dream because of fear? Fear and insecurity are the same thing. When you allow fear to dictate your decisions, you are empowering those fears and insecurities to start a raging fire. Insecurities and fear are a direct result on why we became so deep into drugs.

Being vulnerable is when you were willing to face your addiction head on. Being vulnerable is when you're willing to talk to others about something you don't even like talking to yourself about. What were once thoughts you ignored, now become words that you speak. Vulnerability is the most powerful form of expression you can have.

Being vulnerable shows you that you care about your life. I have said, "I don't give a fuck," a thousand times. Nine hundred and ninety-five of those *were a lie*. We could twist the words into believing that we're not worried about our insecurities anymore and that's what we're leaving behind. Our attitude could be, "Fuck those insecurities and fuck my past. I'm willing to be vulnerable and take chances now." That is one way of looking at being vulnerable. But what I believe to be true to my sobriety is acknowledging that I do care about my insecurities. I have insecurities every day. I will have insecurities for the rest of my life. Instead of continuing this false sense of tough guy, I'd rather embrace my logical self with compassion and honesty.

When you practice all the different concepts in this book, you'll see that you're heading toward the world of mastering your true self.

Exercise

No matter what your insecurities are, write down every single one of them. As you look at that list, analyze, one-by-one, how you can improve on that insecurity. Be honest with yourself in situations where you're being the safe you versus the real you. At times you might not speak up in a group setting because of fear of judgment. At times you might not try new things, like yoga or meditation, because you fear what your friends will say. Identify those moments and go for the real you. You'll never know if you don't try. It's the not knowing that will haunt you for years to come. Be vulnerable.

Chapter 14

Passion

There is a fine line between love and hate, and that's *passion*. Passion isn't necessarily a positive thing. When you're truly passionate about something, you will do anything to achieve it. I was unbelievably passionate about getting drugs every single day. But, I have also been unbelievably passionate about my recovery.

With sobriety, I'm becoming more and more in touch with my emotions. I'm an extremist, and I'm still trying to find the middle ground with a lot of things. Passion is one of them. I frequently start out loving something, but often end up hating it. I've discovered that when I'm able to find balance in things, I'm more rational. If you can be passionate and rational then you've unlocked an important door.

When I was a kid, I fell in love with baseball. There was something about the game that was fascinating to me. I would play with neighborhood friends, in the backyard by myself, and collected as many baseball cards as I could. But when it came to organized baseball, something just didn't fit. My self-esteem as a player just wasn't there. The fact was, I just wasn't any good at the game. Being so young, I lost interest and lost my drive to get better.

I excelled at soccer, but wasn't as passionate about it as I was with football. My passion for football felt like a religion. The problem was that my parents wouldn't allow me to play football until I got to high school. Their worry at the time was injuries at a young age—and they were right. They knew I was an accident-prone little maniac from birth. By the end of my football-playing days, I had broken seven bones, had four different surgeries, separated each shoulder over eight times, and suffered many concussions (at the time I played, they weren't a concern).

My love of football taught me determination. I hated the thought of not being able to do something I desired. I was passionate about challenging myself to be the best. I ate, breathed, slept, and thought about football every single day. Being the very best at the game was my goal.

When I played football for a Junior College in San Diego, we went up to Compton Junior college for a road game. All game long I was second string as a running back, but the first-string player wasn't getting the necessary yards. In the fourth quarter, we were up by a touchdown and wanted to run out the clock for the last couple minutes. We couldn't do that if we weren't getting first downs. My offensive coordinator grabbed me by the mask and said, "The next time we get the ball, I'm putting you in. If you don't get us first downs, then you will never get the opportunity to take the starting spot again. This is it for you." Hell yeah! I had been waiting for that moment. When we got the ball back, I went out onto the field with the starting unit. Adrenaline was flowing. My eyes looked like a wild animal finding its prey and ready to pounce. I heard, "White boy, white rice, Casper, Wonder Bread, powder," and death threats from the crowd as well as the players.

All I could think was to get first downs. The first play was to me. I made a couple of guys miss and got a first down. And then I did it again the next play, and the next. We eventually threw a pass to our star receiver and scored another touchdown. Then won the game!

As we were shaking hands with the opposing team, several of them hugged me, giving me praise for my efforts. I love that about sports. I didn't take those death threats seriously, nor did I take the racial slurs offensive. That story is a great example of when you work so hard for something, and finally get your chance to prove your worth, you rise to the occasion.

Over the years of sobriety, I think about that story, and how I was prepared for that moment. Being prepared allowed me to have *healthy hope*. I say healthy hope because sometimes hope can be harmful. I hope this slot machine hits the jackpot. I hope my landlord stops asking for that rent I'm late on. I hope my car doesn't run out of gas. That's why being fully prepared for something allows destiny to respond appropriately to your calls of hope. In that story, I hoped for a chance. When it came, I took full advantage of it and fulfilled my destiny. In that moment, I had healthy hope and I was fully prepared.

I researched anxiety over the years because it's been in my face throughout my recovery. Numerous times, I've come across the idea that anxiety and excitement are the same, which led me to believe that I've put so much pressure on myself over the years that I work myself into a frenzy. On the one hand is the feeling of accomplishing something, which equals excitement. I find myself conflicted because I've always believed I was supposed to be doing something more with my life, but instead I'm met with my own insecurities and self-doubt. On the other hand, anxiety would start to kick in and I found myself confused, emotionally. I often ended up feeling depressed, then exhausted. I force my thoughts back to doing more with my life, which then led to excitement. The back-and-forth battle between anxiety and excitement started to make sense to me emotionally. I started to recognize that my thoughts have the power to control these two emotions. If I can practice the power of thought when anxiety starts to hit, then I can channel that self-doubt to a place of acceptance. Accepting self-doubt just means that you are acknowledging that you're feeling insecure, but you refuse to let it win.

The obvious dilemma is that when you're passionate about anything, you're walking on a tightrope. At some point you're going to fall on one side or the other. One side is filled with pillows that look like clouds, and the other side is filled with barbed-wire and thumb tacks.

At the foundation of my sobriety is passion, enthusiasm, and optimism. I've been so passionate about my sobriety, and the focus it takes every day, that I end up getting overly passionate about it. I feel the same passion for other addicts as well. And if you're in my life, and not an addict, I have high expectations for you as well. Those closest to me know that I can be overbearing. I'll make you feel like nothing you do is good enough. I don't do that to be mean or degrading, I do it because I'm passionate about life and I believe there's always room for improvement. I have high expectations for myself, as well as those around me. My passion for life changed dramatically when I was in rehab and realized how close to death I got. Because of that experience, I now have this endless amount of passion, enthusiasm, and optimism for life in recovery. Why would I ever allow these words and thoughts to go unspoken? Why would I not try my best to inspire those around me? I'm trying to help motivate and inspire others to meet their true potential.

Once you really start traveling down the path of discovering some of the little things that spark your inner fire, you'll find that path a smooth journey into the world of positive passion. On the flip side, keep in mind how quickly your passion can turn into negativity. Controlling those emotions allows you to maintain your positive passion.

I believe that we are all passionate about a variety of things. We care for starving children and animals, homeless people, and the list goes on. Some of the bigger issues in humanity have yet to be truly dealt with. We need creative thinkers to think outside the box and come up with better ways to address these issues. There's a variety of people trying to come up with plans to clean up the oceans. That's their passion. My belief is that addicts have the solutions to these problems. But we can't be of any service if we don't take care of ourselves first. When addicts obsess over anything that they're passionate about, they will find the solution to any given problem. When addicts start to believe in themselves and find what they're passionate about, then this world will be a better place. I truly believe that addicts will change the world for the better. I will continue to help addicts for the remainder of my days and do everything in my power to help them find their passion.

Passion and excitement should lead to enthusiasm for life. Passion doesn't necessarily mean you're going to be successful because you have it. Passion is simply an energy that you can use to drive you to your destination.

Exercise

One of the key factors to having positive passion is to be able to answer the question, "What do you want out of life?" I'm not asking you to think up some deep crazy thought. I'm asking you to consider something small. It doesn't have to be something huge or earth-shaking; it can be a variety of things.

Think long and hard about what it is you're passionate about. Whatever it is, take the time, make the effort, and never give up. Every single addict who is reading this—you matter. I want you to find your passion and help change the world.

Chapter 15
Leap of Faith

With our new sobriety, we need to be cautious and safe with the decisions we make. Once we've discovered a foundation of sobriety, and have a healthy daily routine, I encourage you to try new things like healthy eating, exercise, leisure time. When you've accomplished a variety of smaller leaps, you'll then try bigger leaps. At times, you won't get the results you hoped for, but you'll accept it because you know you tried. Every month, I average one "leap of faith" moment—from small to big, I commit to taking a chance on just one thing. Taking a leap of faith means you are taking a chance. You believe in yourself, and the end result. It also means you accept the possibility of failure. So frequently we have self-doubt. We allow our thoughts and fears to tell us, stop, no and don't. When you start to visualize yourself achieving a goal, you start to believe it. So, with a leap of faith can you make chance possible? The obvious answer is yes. When you work hard toward anything, you create more possibility. When the doors of possibility are open, you created the possibility for chance, you earned it. You worked hard to open the door to possibilities, which created chance, and chance was created by your persistence. You did all of this by taking a leap of faith.

The most potent aspect to taking a leap of faith is the acceptance of failure. Throughout my life I've had moments where I attempted to avoid failure. I've tried to avoid embarrassment by making decisions based off doing things the safe way. By playing it safe, I can avoid the possibility of failure. In recovery, to be successful, we must accept the good and the bad that we encounter. If we don't, the bad will consume us and take us back to the world of addiction. Accepting failure shows emotional toughness. Once you have that, then taking a leap of faith becomes a part of the real you—the authentic you. In the game of life, play the real you, not the safe you.

As addicts, our biggest leap of faith was going to rehab. Imagine a line graph where you have a baseline of X, which is at zero. When you're addicted to drugs, everything you do is in the negative. Every move you make is a negative number. With time, that number continues to go further and further down the graph below the X line. One day, something in you makes you understand the trendline in your life graph is only going down. That's when you decide to address your addiction. Maybe this moment comes during an intervention, a confrontation with a family member or friend, someone got pregnant; or maybe you wound up in a hospital bed after an overdose, like me. That's when you made the leap of faith. You had the courage to say, "Fuck it. I'll try it. I don't think it's going to work, but I'll try it." That takes so much courage when you're addicted to drugs.

Let's go back to the graph. With that decision, you bring yourself back to baseline—back to zero. The baseline represents doing all right in life: you're not rich, you're not homeless; you're not working your dream job, but you are working and staying sober. For a lot of people, that's great for the rest of their life. I admire anyone willing to take that leap of faith into sobriety.

But what if there's more if you just took another *leap of faith*? There you are at baseline: you've been sober for years, and you want to think about your dream job. Why not take that leap of faith to go for your vision of a better life? When you made the decision to get help for your issues, you put your faith in yourself and your possibilities. There was no way you were ever going to get sober. But something happened. Something came over you. Something allowed you to say, "Fuck it, I'm jumping." Why would you not do the same thing for your dream?

On that line graph, think about the distance you covered to get that deep in the negative. Now, think about the most successful people in the world. Their line graph skyrocketed to success. The distance they covered with their hard work and dedication to their craft is the same distance you covered with your addiction and bad decision-making. If you can go from being that deep in the negative with your addiction, back to baseline with sobriety, then what's holding you back from skyrocketing to the top of your graph? The distance you covered to get sober is the same distance they covered to get success. The answer is taking a leap of faith.

When we take a leap of faith, we are creating distance between our old identity, and our new one. Taking a leap of faith has everything to do with distancing ourselves from insecurities. One of the greatest emotions you can feel in recovery is by shedding off those layers of self-doubt. Ridding yourself of that scared individual, who ran to drugs to cope. That old identity was scared to take a leap of faith, and instead turned to drugs. Recovery is that opportunity to have a second chance at that moment: those moments where you did nothing because of fear of failure; those moments you wished you could have back. Recovery, if you choose to see it this way, is a magical opportunity that allows you to identify where you went wrong, and how to avoid repeating the same behaviors. Taking a leap of faith is taking control of your life. You make the decision no matter the outcome. If the outcome ends in failure, then at least you learn from it. It's the not knowing because you didn't try that leads back to the old you. Shedding off those layers of self-doubt will provide you with a feeling drugs never gave you.

There's something to be said about you being willing to give sobriety a chance. Even though none of us were one hundred percent sold on rehab, we gave it a chance. Even though we were scared, frightened, and exposed, we took that leap. I strongly believe that every day in recovery is a testament to that leap, to that belief.

Overcoming your addiction showed you your potential. Look at the process you went through to get sober. You learned some shit. You think you won't learn when you take a leap of faith at your dream? You will make mistakes while pursuing it. But, having the courage to leap, you've been there done that. It's doable. Once you do that, what happens to that line graph? You flip those numbers upside down. That's what addicts do, we take chances, we take leaps, and we achieve what we desire. We're just doing it sober now.

This book is a leap for me. I want to help other addicts. I don't have all the answers, but if I don't take this leap of faith with this book, then these words go unspoken.

I very much believe in the art of mastering what you desire. I set out to master sobriety. I researched people who I admired, who encountered adversity and became successful because of it. I read articles, watched videos, and searched for what made them achieve the impossible. Out of all those individuals, every one of them, this was my favorite common denominator; *they were willing to do the things no one else was willing to do.*

Ask any drug addict what they were willing to

do to get their drugs. Most won't even answer that question because of embarrassment, shame, and regret. As addicts we did some nasty, fucked-up, dirty shit. Your physical frame, and your mental state, is capable of things you had no idea you could do. Just because it was for an addiction doesn't negate the fact that you're capable of doing the same ambitious things sober. That means your ability to make a leap of faith is just as strong, if not stronger, than the most successful people in the world. Obviously, your leap will now be for your success. Your leap won't have a risk factor of prison or death. Your leap is to happiness and equanimity.

Desire + Belief = Achievement every single time.

We've all had experiences where we desired something, believed we could get it, and we achieved getting it. When you truly desire something, you have an urgency come over you. You fixate on the thing you desire, and then start plotting on how you can obtain it. Once you find yourself thinking of all the different ways you can get it, you start to believe you can make this happen. When you believe you can, you'll achieve it every time.

Here's an example: You desire a candy bar. The more you think about it, the more you want it. You think about the cash in your wallet, your car, and how quickly you can go make this happen. You desired a candy bar, you believed you could get it because you have money and transportation. In that moment, you have the strong desire, the belief to go get it, so you can now go achieve it.

Here's another example: I had a roommate in college who didn't have any cash on him, ever, and needed to borrow $2.00 so he could go get a beer. At the time, $1.99 could get you a cheap 40 ounces. So, I allowed him to go through my change jar. After a couple weeks of this, he had used all my quarters, dimes, and nickels. I thought that was the end of it, but sure enough he came over and asked if he could get my pennies. This man counted out one hundred and ninety-nine pennies and went off to the store. No shame to his game. Why? Because he desired something, believed he could do it, so he did just that.

Addicts use this equation every day of their addiction. We desired our drugs, believed we could get it, and achieved getting it. Out of the three words (desire, belief, achievement), which one of these words is most likely to hurt us? Some people think desire when I ask this. Some people think achievement. But what I'm truly getting at is the *power of belief.* So frequently we are frightened to take chances because we don't believe in ourselves. We desire a promotion, but we don't think we'll get it, so we don't bother trying. Believing in yourself is the key. When we desire more in our lives post-recovery, we feel an urgency to achieve that. But when we don't believe in ourselves, we become stagnant. No one else is going to help. No one else is going to do the work for you. When you accept you need to believe in yourself, your character grows in tremendous ways.

I struggled with road rage. So, a small leap of faith was to be overly nice to everyone on the road. I did it, and it helped change my attitude. It's not perfect, but it helped for the most part. Another example is applying for jobs that you desire, but you're scared of rejection. If you don't try, you'll never know. Taking a leap of faith might not always work in your favor, but at least you tried.

Call me crazy, but when this opioid epidemic brings out an array of successful former addicts, remember what I'm saying here.

Exercise

Make a list of small leaps of faith you can make today. Don't do anything that might cause injury or harm to yourself or others. What positive changes can you make that will surprise yourself—challenge you to become a better you? This exercise is intended for you to follow your heart and nothing more. Make writing out a list of things you need to try, a monthly thing. This helped me feel excitement in my recovery. I hope it provides the same for you.

Chapter 16

Leadership

Good leaders help us maximize our potential and bring out our capabilities. They inspire us to be better than we currently are. Great leaders bring out our greatest qualities. My favorite form of leadership is leading by example. Leaders are generally respected for their ability to take charge and know exactly what needs to be done when no one else will. By taking charge and getting things done, it sets the tone for everyone who's observing.

Integrity is key to great leadership. It means doing the right thing, even when no one is watching. The people I admire most in the world are the ones who demonstrate integrity even when they don't feel like it. If I see someone pick up trash outside of the store and take it to a trash can, then I'm more likely to do that same action. They're making an effort for the greater good of humanity. That's a beautiful thing to practice. Sure, it feels great to be recognized for your efforts. I love recognition from others. But, in my years of sobriety, I'm discovering it feels even better to do good things and not worry about the recognition. I feel good just knowing I'm doing the right thing.

Every day, I try to do something good. With these daily behaviors, I'm leading myself to the future me—the guy I aspire to be. My visualization of success takes this daily discipline to strengthen my character. I'm leading my scared, insecure self to a place of contentment.

When it comes to the mind of an addict, the only leadership you truly trust is within yourself. Obviously in this book, I've talked a lot about there being two sides to us: the good and bad. The line between good and evil runs right through our soul. Being a good leader consists of us accepting that.

When you devote yourself to a life of sobriety, you are capable of being a leader. When you find yourself with a healthful morning routine, structure in your day, and discipline in your every decision, then you have leadership qualities. Remind yourself how hard you've worked to gain a healthy understanding of your addiction. You're capable of conquering so much. The mere fact that you are in recovery shows courage within you. That shows that you're willing to take charge of your life and your situation. Remind yourself of all the hard work it took to get to this very moment. When you give yourself recognition for your efforts, you start to realize that you are the one in control. Your entire addiction consisted of not having control.

When you strive to be a good leader within

yourself, you will experience the voice of insecurity: "Stop, no, don't! We're going to be judged. We're going to be criticized. Don't do this." I will never allow that voice to influence me, to be less than what I'm intended to be. I am destined for greatness, happiness, and an ability to recognize my addiction as a gift. That's me being my own leader.

Throughout my life I admired good leaders, but I've had a lot of bad ones, too. The easiest way to spot the bad ones was by observing their selfish ways. How many of you have witnessed a boss do things that makes them look good, and others bad? How many times have you witnessed a boss do the bare minimum, and take the easy route, instead of being the hardest worker in the company? A lot of people in the world of work want to do the bare minimum and get paid well for it. The biggest question is, do you think your boss cares about what's in the best interest of the company? I ask that question because a lot of bosses will get into a position of power and stop caring.

I've seen people who lead by fear. I've feared some of my bosses over the years because I liked my job and didn't want to lose it. A lot of bosses have deep insecurities about their job position, and they doubt themselves. Because of their insecurities, they have to make it look as if they're important. Making employees feel as if their job is on the line, and making them feel fear allows the boss to feel as if he/she is important and significant. Anytime I witnessed this behavior in bosses I felt disappointed. They were hired to help the company blossom, and instead their own insecurities got in the way, and now the company is average or worse.

I've feared good leaders because I didn't want to disappoint them. I worked hard to earn their trust and respect because I trusted and respected them. I feared them being disappointed in me. When I think of my favorite leaders, I think of great bosses or sports coaches. When you come across a good leader, you're willing to take a bullet for them. You're willing to do whatever it is they ask of you because your respect for them is so high. Those are the types of leaders I fear disappointing. I want to impress them because of my respect for them. I fear that look on their face if I affect them negatively by my actions. Actually, that's a good fear to have. It motivates me to be the best I can, every day.

In order to succeed in recovery, we need to think like a leader. This is where we as addicts need to take responsibility for every action we display, every comment that we make, and every move we make.

What's important to figure out now is, what kind of leader are you? Good leaders show loyalty. Good leaders show that they care about, and value, the team. People bounce from job to job because they're in search of a good leader. Those same people want to feel a sense of purpose within the team. When the leader simply shows up, does the bare minimum, and shows a lack of support to the company, then relapse is moments away.

You Are the CEO of *You*

You are the CEO of your company. This company is you: your mind, body, and emotions. Because you're the CEO, you need to take full responsibility for anything and everything that goes wrong. That's a part of sobriety—taking responsibility for your actions. You can either run a good company, or you can let your company go to shit. Within this company, you have a Human Resources department, maintenance, billing, etc.

Human Resources is responsible for your integrity, mindset, work ethic, and any mental issues that come up. When you allow HR to lose sight of your positive mental attitude, that's when your daily thoughts become rage, anger, and depression. If that happens, your thoughts can spiral out of control, and relapse is waiting. If HR doesn't do its job, then you have a problem handling your day-to-day responsibilities.

Maintenance deals with the plumbing, electricity, and the overall health of your body—the building. Maintenance is your food intake, exercise, and how you treat your body. When you let the plumbing, electricity, and the overall health of the building go, what do you expect to happen? That's when you get fat, out of shape, and your self-esteem goes to shit. If that happens, your building starts to crumble—you get physically worse. That means relapse is waiting at the door like a debt collector.

Billing deals with finances and the daily responsibilities that come with giving and receiving, being financially responsible, and an attentiveness to details. When the billing department doesn't stay focused on the income flow, the money dries up, your hard work fades, and you're in financial ruin. If that happens, relapse is waiting for you to spend your last penny on your addiction, instead of what really matters.

CEOs do the right thing for the sake of the company, even if that means they lose something for the time being. They put their ego aside and base their decisions off what's best for the company. They make business decisions, not emotional decisions. Good CEOs get right in the mix of the shit and are willing to do the dirty-work if need be. Good CEOs know exactly what's going on within the company, and know everyone's job, from the custodian to accounting and HR.

Your Priority List

As a leader for yourself, what's most important to you every day? What comes first? Is it responsibilities, family, friends, pets, your job, or what? Every decision I make is important for the same reason. My priority list consists of doing the things that I see as beneficial for my daily objective, maintaining my sobriety.

Because of my addiction, my priority list has changed. My mental and physical health comes before I deal with anyone else. After that, who I interact with is very important, too. To be a good leader, you want to surround yourself with people who want to grow within themselves, as well as see you grow. You can surround yourself with a quantity of people, but what I'm suggesting is that you find quality people instead. Quality interactions lead to quality actions. Every interaction per day is important because it plays a role in my sobriety.

I have spent so much time and energy on my sobriety over the years that I question if I'm obsessed with getting better as a human being. The answer is yes! I accept that I have an addictive personality. I accept that I obsess over things. I also respect that some of those things need balance. But, when it comes to my priority list, it's non-fucking-negotiable. Training your brain to set a goal, and make that goal non-negotiable, is a matter of discipline. When I started mapping out a priority list, I set out to make it reasonable, logical, and peppered with an attitude of obsession.

The single most impactful decision that I put on my priority list is my mentality. What's my perspective toward my day? Do I have a positive or shitty attitude going on within my mind? Spending time on gathering my thoughts has been the most important aspect to my priority list. The greatest way to do that is by meditation. Obviously, you aren't going to be able to traipse off in the middle of your work-day, so you need to schedule that in, regularly. At first, you'll struggle to have order within your own thoughts. Then you're going to struggle to achieve your priority list.

If meditation is not your thing, at least have a strategy to keep an open, positive mind during the day. Another strategy is to do self-check-in some-time in your day. Are you having a productive day? This helps you keep you on track.

This list can be whatever you want it to be, and can be changed every day if you want to do that. The objective is to set yourself up for success and avoid relapse. It is always the little things you do that matter most. All the subtle little moves you make each day, are the most important ones. Write down, or take a mental note, on the things that worked best. What are the things that are keeping you motivated and inspired for each day?

Every time you think about leadership, think of yourself. The fact that you made an effort to get clean shows an enormous amount of leadership on your part. Don't forget that you are the CEO of you. Take ownership in that and take responsibility for everything you do.

Exercise

Write out a full day of things that you want to accomplish that are basic daily living skills, respon-sibilities, and things that will be a benefit to your sobriety. Map out what your very first move is for the day. What is the first thing you do when you get out of bed? I force myself to make the bed, and I dislike doing it every time. Now you want to map out what you're having for breakfast. What you ingest will have an impact on your day. As you write out a full day of things, make sure to include things that you don't necessarily want to do, but you know you need to do; exercise being an example. Little things like cleaning up the garage, doing the dishes, and laundry, are basic daily living skills. What's on your list?

Chapter 17

Self-Care

Self-care consists of three aspects: the physical, the mental, and the emotional. Taking care of ourselves physically means we control the food we eat, our activity level per day, and hygiene. Taking care of ourselves mentally consists of a willingness to learn, coping with stress, and who we spend time with. When we take care of ourselves emotionally, we express ourselves, discover what inspires us to stay sober, and find happiness in each day. All three aspects have everything to do with the success of our sobriety, but they also have everything to do with what it is to be human. Keep in mind that these three things intermingle.

The Physical

Eating Right: One of the most important aspects of being physically healthy is the food we eat. When we're in recovery, it can sometimes be hard to eat healthy food. Food feels like one of the only things you can still enjoy without having to go back to rehab. So take it in stages. Every week implement something healthy into your daily intake. As a sober man, I analyze every detail of my day. I put a lot of emphasis on my food intake as I try to add healthy choices to my lifestyle changes. I'm still doing a lot of searching regarding how and what foods affect me. It's funny how my addiction was illegal and socially unacceptable, but processed foods are acceptable and a part of the way we eat in this country. One is legal, the other illegal; both are killing people every day.

Since I stopped drinking alcohol, I've discovered a dramatic difference in my body. Over time, I mapped out what my daily life was like as a drinker. To start my day off, I would drink Gatorade, thinking it would help with the hangover. The food I consumed throughout the day was either fast-or processed foods. Once evening came, I would drink at least four 40-ounce bottles of beer, topped off with my biggest meal of the day. After that, I headed straight to bed.

At that point in my life, I did not care about my wellbeing. I was a drinker and didn't give a fuck about life or death. In my mind, I was indestructible. Beer hits your system and gives you that buzz, that euphoric feeling. Then the next day, you're left feeling run-down and sort of soggy. But still, that night, you do it all over again.

I discovered a similar thing with soda pop. When I found myself getting hungover from sodas I decided to research the effects of sugar. Between the caffeine and the sugar in soda, I was having to urinate a lot, which led to me being dehydrated. When I stopped the sodas and increased my water intake, I noticed an increase in energy. Ultimately that's what we're after, to feel more energy. The difference between beer and water is the quick effects versus patience. With water, I feel it the next day. The days I don't drink a lot of water, I'm dragging ass. I drink water with the attitude that it will give me a euphoric feeling the next day.

Let's focus on the frozen food section for a moment. How many times have you eaten microwavable foods from the frozen food section, thinking it's a quick and easy meal? As a consumer, I was sold on the protein in chicken fingers, plus they are easy to make, microwavable, and they taste good. I trusted that the food industry was being honest and not cutting this product down, and that it would get me the nutrients I need to maintain a healthy lifestyle. When you research these products, you discover products like these are anything but healthy. In fact, they are quite the opposite. (Hint: don't eat the chicken strips!)

The people/corporations making these foods are no different than a drug dealer. They know you'll be back: you're an addict, you're predictable. They cut these foods down, add shit that our bodies aren't meant to eat, and ensure there's something about this product that makes you want more. The food industry has highly intelligent people behind their marketing schemes.

Just because the label says gluten-free, high in protein, high in fiber and vitamins, that doesn't mean it's *actually* healthy. Read the ingredients and understand what's in that package. The food industry will do everything they possibly can to get you hooked on their product, and keep you coming back for more. This is no different than the addiction issues we're already dealing with.

I exercise consistently and need the proper nutrients to maintain my health. When I eat processed foods, like those frozen chicken strips, I don't feel good. It gets me by, but it doesn't fulfill me. I can feel the difference in raw foods versus cut-down processed foods. These days, I eat kale and spinach for breakfast most mornings. I drink water, and only water, six days a week. With sobriety, I've discovered through a lot of trial and error that the things I consume will affect me immediately. I know the foods I'm eating are good for me because I feel a thousand times different than I did while eating processed foods. When I eat fresh vegetables and fruits, and hormone-free meats, I feel healthy. The good foods are like Oxycontin to an addict, I know what I'm getting, and it gets the job done every time. Processed foods are like heroin: they're cut down, and you're unsure of what you're going to get.

Exercise: This doesn't have to mean going to the gym. You have so many options for physical activity that you can choose from: swimming, biking, hiking, running, walking, yoga, basketball, softball, etc. What's great about choosing one or several of these is finding enjoyment out of it. Some people like lifting weights and going to the gym by themselves. Others want to have a friend to help push them. No matter what route you choose, there is a level of discomfort.

Exercise will work your lungs, cause muscle fatigue and soreness, and make you feel pretty tired at first. Research activities and find some that appeal to you and have fun with your exercise. Once you get started with an activity, you'll find that it's a daily must in your routine.

Hygiene: How you treat yourself plays a role in your sobriety. Every day, shower and brush your teeth. Clipping your finger- and toenails, grooming your hair and facial hair (if you have it) are basics. More intense hygiene might include getting a massage, getting a pedicure, and taking time out just to get rest. Show yourself that you care about yourself.

For years I struggled with foot odor. Over my years of sobriety, I have increased how frequently I wash my feet, change my socks, and don't wear the same pair of shoes every day.

Maybe that sounds basic to you. I recognized a problem where I needed to be better to myself. I needed to show more care toward my hygiene.

During my years as an addict, I didn't give a shit about my teeth. Through my years of dysfunction, I developed an ugly tooth, my brother-in-law called it a poop tooth. You know the type, that one tooth that is more yellow than the rest of them. It brought me a lot of shame and embarrassment. I tried pretending it didn't bother me, but I was insecure about it. I also didn't floss. Because of that bad tooth, I didn't see much of a point in doing it. Of course, this led to more trouble with my teeth. It took some years before I finally stopped being so stubborn about flossing. Once I started taking care of myself, I went to the dentist. They were able to help me understand how to better take care of my teeth, and even improve the looks of the ugly one.

That brings up another topic: *doctors in general.* Now that you're on the path to wellness, go and get a physical. You've decided to be healthy and stick around, a physician can help you get there. Take the physical, then go annually for your check-up— you've been abusing your body, and it's likely it has left a trail of destruction. If you're over 50, get a colonoscopy. Those who have abused alcohol are far more likely to develop colon cancer or other intestinal disorders.

I have struggled with *sleep* since puberty. My thoughts race and I struggle to calm my mind. I thought for years that by drinking all evening long, then having a big meal before bed, that's how I could get good sleep. Through years of sobriety, healthy eating, and exercise, I've been able to get better sleep. I still struggle at times, but it is better. Exercising helped me mentally, physically, and emotionally. By the end of my day, I am ready for sleep because of the exercise. The main thing I noticed was eliminating meals before bed. I started sleeping a lot better after that. Another thing is to avoid drinking water hours before bed. When you wake up periodically throughout the night to use the bathroom, it disrupts your ability to sleep solidly. Sobriety helped more than anything. I don't remember sleeping well during my addiction—ever. Not hammering my body with toxins helped me be able to live an all-around healthier lifestyle. Sobriety, exercise, and eating healthy helped transform my sleep. With good sleep I'm more likely to be focused and ready for each day.

You're going to hate this next one, but I am a total advocate for *cold showers.* In my research of successful people, I came across Wim Hof, who's an advocate for cold baths for the abundance of health benefits. If you have zero desire to do this, I understand, but still research this guy because he is fascinating. When it comes to physically, mentally, and emotionally strengthening myself, nothing comes close to the impact cold showers have had on me.

Having been an addict, I am always looking for a challenge. I thought about the time my dealer told me to use an ice cube if he turned blue. I thought about the time I tried to drink a cold beer in my rear. I was frightened to try this cold shower thing, but I'd already done worse things.

I was excited at the possible health benefits that it's supposed to provide. Well, for the first three months I sang at the top of my lungs to help cope. I do this shower every morning for three to five minutes. No excuses.

Clean Your Room! Your environment is as important as your body, and is part of your hygiene. Go to your bedroom/apartment/house and really look around. Is it a mess—cluttered and disorganized? Get cleaning supplies and clean it to the best of your ability. Organize everything to your liking. What is it that you don't really need? Be honest with yourself. Most of us have things that we've been holding onto for years. These can be items that are sentimental, remind us of good memories, or sometimes we don't really know where it came from. Get rid of the shit that you don't use, don't admire, and don't care for anymore. After the big clean up, look at your space. If you've done a thorough job, it will now be clean, healthy, filled with positivity, and filled with things that truly matter. This is another aspect of creating a better you.

Some of those little things that we neglected during our years of drugs and alcohol can now be changed. You will feel a change in your physical health. Treat yourself differently than you have in the past. You'll find it will make a great deal of difference to you.

Putting it all together: Get a calendar specifically for your accomplishments physically. You're going to write down what you did every day, never taking a day off. You might workout one day, then go for a walk the second day. The next two days you eat veggies as a snack instead of chips. Fifth day comes and you decide to do meditation and yoga. Sixth day you clip your toenails. Seventh day, you attempt the cold shower. Every single day you make an effort toward tending to yourself physically.

Mental Health

There's a strong connection between working on your mental health and your wellbeing. I've learned a variety of healthy ways to cope with stress in my years of sobriety. I had to research those ways—I had to work for it—but in the end, I've enjoyed everything I've discovered. I have also made a lot of effort with who I spend time with, and who to avoid.

Visualization: I have discovered the beautiful me that I always wanted to be. One of the keys was through visualization. When I was in rehab, I had daydreams of being successful spiritually and financially. I saw that future-me doing great things in the years to come. I've been chasing that dude ever since. Chasing my future self was probably the smartest move I made mentally in my sobriety. I had to search and discover who I wanted to be first, then I started the great chase. That trek from visualizing who I wanted to be. But that all started from me learning new things.

When I was in first grade, my parents had me tested for hearing issues due to my inability to focus and pay attention in class. The teachers noticed that I would stare off into another dimension and struggled to return. After the tests were complete, the doctor reported to my parents that I could hear just fine—but I was a world-class daydreamer. My ability to travel so many different places while sitting at my desk was—in my mind—a gift.

When I would visualize being successful, I would see myself finding a better way to do something and accomplishing it. If I could visualize scoring touchdowns, and making crazy moves on the football field, then I believed it. It wasn't just sports that I saw this, it was me getting better at talking to girls, at being able to lift more weight, getting my license as a teenager, and that sort of thing. The list goes on throughout my life.

Your *perspective*, your outlook, allows you to visualize. Imagining your goals leads you to strategize. If you make the effort to improve the value of your food intake, and picturing yourself getting better, you'll be healthier. You believe this will work. You now see yourself in shape, with more energy, and accomplishing things you currently are not accomplishing. That's the visualization. Then to make that visualization concrete, you put all the elements in motion: you research healthy foods, what exercise works for you, and discover how to create a healthy mindset. So, you do that. That's the strategy. This all starts with your perspective. If you question the process, and think it might not work, then you're correct, it won't work. If your perspective is that it *will* work, then you're correct, it will.

When I was addicted, and also in rehab, I visualized being successful with sobriety. I envisioned myself never drinking or using drugs ever again. I envisioned myself being sincerely happy every day for the rest of my life. I envisioned meeting the girl of my dreams. I envisioned being successful without a lot of money. I envisioned all of that and then some. Currently, I am on-track to achieving all I imagined for myself. But it takes work to make it happen.

Stress: The number one thing that I stress about more than anything is the things that I can't control. I get stressed about the possibility of what someone might say to me. And if they do, I stress about what I'll say in return. Work can be stressful. Relationships can be stressful. No matter how much stress you take on per day, how much of it is totally out of your control? When I started to practice identifying the things that were causing stress, I was then able to decide if I could fix it or not. If I could not fix it, then it was time to move on to a different thought.

We all know that *exercise* can help relieve stress. *Eating, yoga*, and *meditation* can also help. But nothing is more important than addressing your *mental state*. One of the quick tricks I like to use is music. Music has helped me get out of my head countless times. Finding music that you enjoy, and that helps you think positive thoughts, can be a quick trick to get out of your negative state of thinking. If you find yourself stressed, but you don't have access to music, play the song in your head. Sing the lyrics in your head.

Another little trick that I use is to take a *deep breath* in for four full seconds, then exhale for another four full seconds. I do that a few times. The inhale/exhale thing seems small, but has helped me tremendously in my sobriety.

My last little trick is to *focus on body parts*. Focus all your energy and concentration on your toes. When you stare at your toes and give your undivided attention to them, you mentally feel them. Then move to your feet, calves, knees, thighs, hips, stomach, shoulders, neck, head, and then your fingers. When you give all your energy to doing this, you release stress.

Keeping Positive: If keeping positive was easy, then everyone would be positive all the time. We all want to be positive, but then life happens. What I've learned over the years is that when I get upset, or frustrated, I quickly try to change that state of mind.

Similar to music, or breathing techniques, I try to think about how *grateful* I am that I don't have to go through withdrawals today. I also think about what it was like to be stuck in the loop of addiction. Thinking about how bad I once had it. This helps me look at today as a beautiful day. The true test is making an effort to focus on positive thinking versus negative.

Once you start going deep into negative thinking, it's hard to get out. Be ready to fight and see it as a fight. This is a mental boxing match between your negative thoughts and your positive thoughts. When you're able to practice being positive during adversity, you're then better equipped for everything life throws your way.

Educate Yourself: Everyone has their own way of learning and what works best for them. I suggest reading. I don't even like reading, but every time I do it, I feel sharper. For those of you who prefer watching videos, research whatever it is that you desire to learn. In your upcoming years of sobriety, it's extremely important to stay busy with healthy thoughts. If you don't pursue the better you, then you become complacent. Being complacent can be the death of us as addicts. Keep your mind hungry, keep your mind sharp, and have fun doing what you want to do in your recovery.

Putting it all together: Journal your daily thoughts. Tell how you were brushing your teeth and started getting pissed about how your boss talked to you the day before. Note how you slept the night before. How you felt when waking up. Write down how that guy cut you off in traffic and it really made you upset. Write all of it down. Once you have a full day's worth of your thoughts and reactions, use a red pen and draw a line through the thoughts that were pointless. Then, sit back and look at it. You'll be surprised how frequently you think of stupid, pointless, unproductive thoughts.

Once you cross out those pointless thoughts,

take the time to then admire how many good ones there are left. Your list is filled with things that truly matter. Now your thoughts look clean, healthy, and filled with positivity.

Emotional Health

How we express ourselves every day is a direct reflection of our emotions. That starts by finding things that inspire us and keep us focused on our sobriety. What inspires you to stay sober? What makes you happy in your life without drugs and alcohol? When you find what makes you happy, then you're inspired to go get it. When you realize that, then you express yourself in a manner that consists of who you are, and what you represent. Now, that all sounds great, but most addict's self-esteem in recovery can start out as a challenge. Your emotions can easily lean toward negativity. How to cope with yourself mentally, leads to helping you emotionally. It's a fight.

Sobriety is a very emotional experience, especially in the first year. It's hard to grasp and find what's going to make you happy in sobriety. Focusing positive emotions on each moment shows that you're trying. Every moment that you get through shows that you're trying and that you care. At the end of every day, you get to reflect on getting through it and recognizing, you did it again! Every day that you get through, allows you to build your sober character. Emotionally you're confronting the demon of addiction. You start to believe in yourself because of this. Emotionally, that's a beautiful snowball effect.

The Domino Effect: Small little details can lead to relapse. One false move and you can slip back into the world of addiction. Searching for connection gets you closer to yourself. A big part of your happiness, inspiration, and expression, comes from your thoughts.

Focusing your thoughts and decision-making on positivity is no easy task. It's a daily practice. Look at decision-making that stems from your thoughts as dominos. One row goes down the right path, the other goes down the wrong. When we make decisions we shouldn't act on, we're more likely to knock down the next "negative domino thought" that might lead to relapse or something even worse. When we make good decisions, we're more likely to knock down the next "positive domino thought" that might lead to our success in sobriety. Out of the two rows, which one moves faster? Well, *the wrong row,* of course! Bad outcomes are always easy to find and easy to achieve. Good outcomes take hard work and patience. Practice understanding what sorts of thoughts create the bad domino and learn to avoid them.

Communicate With Others: Something that was scary for me was simply connecting with others: the grocery store clerk, clerks at the bank, job interviews, and just generally "peopling." I remember sweating as I would talk to retail workers because of social anxiety. That was just a part of this new life of sobriety. I started to practice reaching out to others. Here's what I did: went for a walk around town and made sure it was an area where people would be. I attempted making eye-contact with them when they noticed me. I smiled and greeted them with a hello. I did that throughout the walk. I had more people say "hello" back than I expected. Yes, there were people who didn't respond at all. I expected that. The point of doing it though, was to put myself in a new place, where I was interacting with others.

Communicating with others is a huge part of the human experience—one of the greatest spiritual nutrients is connection, finding commonalities with others. Communicating with others helps you grow into a better person. Focusing on those small details like talking to others creates a greater chance at remaining sober for the remainder of your life. As you reach out, you'll find reasons to believe in hope again. This will help you mentally. These are beautiful experiences that you can implement into your new sober life.

Gratitude is the Attitude: Every single day, work toward maintaining a healthy body. I do the same with my mind. My thoughts often take me down a road of frustration and irritability. I need to cancel that bad attitude. They remind me to check myself. I have a beautiful life: I have a good job; a wife who loves me; a car that works; I have a healthy body that works; and I have a mind that is capable of accomplishing whatever I want. More than anything in the world, I'm grateful for my addiction, and my addictive personality. In other words, my new attitude is gratitude. This one new point of view will change your life if you practice it every day. Like everything else though, it takes daily practice.

As addicts we went through the daily life of struggle and pain with our addiction. We went through withdrawals. That's pain, and we know that pain is necessary for success. When you want to get in physical shape, you're going to experience a certain amount of pain to achieve a healthier body. When you want to learn something new and struggle to understand it, you go through a level of mental pain and anguish. When you let go of an unhealthy relationship or friendship, it's bound to cause emotional pain. After experiencing that pain, you have no choice but to let time heal those wounds. It was your ability to endure the pain that led to you feeling euphoria. You'll never appreciate the warmth in gratitude if you haven't experienced the cold in pain.

Finding gratitude after the first couple months of rehab, and letting go of my bitterness, led to success in recovery. Gratitude will change your life if you practice it every day.

Excuses: After years of working on my sobriety, I noticed how excuses were affecting me emotionally. It wasn't a good feeling and I got tired of myself.

When we're addicted, we justify and make excuses for everything we do.

Excuses murder success.

I say those exact words to myself every time I make an excuse for myself. That's helped me immensely when it comes to being in control of my emotions. During my workouts, I'll try to convince myself to avoid certain exercises. First thing that pops into my head, "Excuses murder success," so I end up doing those exact exercises. Even small things like getting the laundry done, doing the dishes, and reading that book I've been meaning to read.

Every time you make an excuse for yourself, identify the excuse, then be honest if it's getting in the way of what you want to achieve. The reason I suggest this one is because I believe it to be a key factor as to why I have never relapsed. When you push yourself to no longer allow excuses to get in the way, then you're doing the opposite of all that justifying and excuse making you did as an addict.

Happiness: Everyone wants to find happiness for themselves in this lifetime. The problem is that we generally spend most our lives looking for it. We end up chasing a life that we believe will make us happy, when in fact, happiness is right in front of us. Happiness is a state of mind. Fear, pain, and suffering feed off of your thoughts. When you feed those emotions, then you feel the fear. To find happiness, you have to fight off any negative thoughts. To feel happiness, you have to feed happiness. When you fear failure, then you tend to believe it. You think about it, you feel it, and you continue the thought. When you think about a positive outcome, and believe in it, then you find happiness. When you feel pain, whether physical or emotional, you can make it worse by your thoughts. You can continue to convince yourself that it won't get better, or you can think positive and mentally work toward tampering down the pain. When you feel emotional suffering, it was your thoughts that led to it being suffering. Something was a small negative thought, then within your mind you exaggerated it into suffering by overthinking it. The only way to get back to happiness is by you and your way of thinking. Happiness is earned by the effort you put forth to attain it. We are all in control of our emotions. Meaning we have the capabilities to control them. But it takes hard work and practice. When you practice anything on a consistent basis, you get better at it. Eventually you either perfect it or get close to perfecting it. To find happiness you must practice happiness.

Work/Life Balance: One of the biggest changes I've made in sobriety is how I spend my time away from work. I work 40 hours a week and make sure that everything I do away from work is constructive and beneficial to my sobriety. I can't express the joy I feel in my personal life. It took work though, because I used to be quite lazy. Look at how we spend our free time. Think about the amount of people you know who don't do shit in their free time away from work. It's good to unwind and relax, but most people don't do anything, and then wonder why things aren't getting better.

Because of our addiction issues, we have a tendency to do things in excess. Taking pride in your work ethic and doing the best job you can is a great quality. But, it's equally important to have the same attitude in your personal life. One of the tricks I've used for years is to debrief with myself about my workday on my drive home. After about ten minutes, it's now time to focus on my personal life. Work can cause a lot of stress for all of us. You will find yourself more productive at work when you have a fresh attitude. That fresh attitude stems from you focusing on your personal life away from work. Finding balance in your work, and your personal life, does take practice. We tend to forget that we go to work so we can enjoy our personal lives.

What matters most is our free time. Allowing work to consume you is destructive to your overall health. In recovery that's the last thing you need.

What I have come to value most in my sobriety is how I value myself first before anyone else. Every single day, I work toward maintaining a healthy body. I do the same with my mind, and because of that, my emotions are in a good place. Being a drug addict has changed my life for the better. I have worked hard over the years to maintain my sobriety.

What strengthens me emotionally is that I earned everything that I've received.

Putting it all together: Go for a walk, lie in bed, sit on the couch, or find a place of comfort. Once you've done that, focus on nothing but thoughts that bring you peace and happiness. By doing this, you're trying to alter your mental state of stress and worry. Even on days you're not feeling stressed and worried, take ten minutes to focus on everything going well in life. Think about things you look forward to. By doing this you learn to look at life with a different attitude. When you can consistently practice being in a positive state of mind, you'll find yourself more frequently in that state.

Chapter 18

Love

Addiction is like your own little community of shit, and you're the mayor. You're stuck in this little town of chaos and you have no idea how to maintain order. Everywhere you look, you see madness and dysfunction. You want to clean the community up, but how? Should we continue the madness in hopes that it will eventually fade? Or should we use love and understanding as to why this is such chaos. No matter how crazy my life has become at times, it was when I felt love in my heart that all my issues dissipated. The best way to clean up the community is love.

Sobriety is an opportunity to leave the town of Addiction for good. The promise of being sober is like a tiny ray of sunshine. And what is that beam of light? Love. That sliver of love is resilient, though. In fact, it never leaves you. That little bit of love has been inside you through the entire time you've been addicted. It just held on, waiting for you to notice it.

When loved ones stage an intervention, or an event happens that triggers your realization that you need to get sober, it's love that leads to recovery. You may not feel that emotion at first—in fact—you may feel the opposite. But what you are experiencing is your family and friends trying to reach that love within you.

I learned to laugh again in rehab. That was the first time I recognized laughter leads back to love. It's a long journey at times, but it helps. Laughter helped me calm the negative thoughts. It was a break from the pain. Those negative thoughts are so thick in rehab that laughter is your drug of choice. When someone makes you laugh, you're able to capture a break from yourself. That break from self opens the door to love. This doesn't happen immediately, it takes time. When you feel love, real love, your life presents more clarity.

When you first venture into recovery, the last thing you feel is love. You're actually looking for clarification as to what just happened in the last years. When you start to smile again, laugh, and cry tears of joy, you're starting to reconnect with the real you. Those moments of laughter and joy start to break up the complications that addiction relentlessly provided. Once that happens, then life starts to become more simplified and has more clarity. It opens the door to more laughter, joy, and smiles. Those little moments of laughter and joy are love re-entering the picture.

When I went to rehab, I wasn't looking for love, but I did love talking to the woman who became my wife. She was consistently funny. Had I met my wife in a dumpster, we would still be together. I can't express how much heroin and alcohol loved me, and how much I loved them back. But my wife's love? She surpassed that with the fluidity of pure peace, grace, and beauty. She is charming like no other. I find myself starstruck at times. I've never enjoyed the company of another the way I do with her. Her mannerisms, her smile, her laugh, are all an exhilarating experience. Her love for others was attractive, too: her daughter, her grandson, her mother, her brothers, her friends, and for my family. And finally, the way she loves me.

But when I met her, her self-love was broken. I've seen her at her worst, and still loved everything about her. Her ability to recognize her own insecurities and accept them is a beautiful sight to see. She loves herself now. She inspires me to love myself. Making her laugh is a daily must. Impressing her is a daily must. We have been on this journey of sobriety together. This journey all started with laughter.

We've discovered that the world is still unforgiving after rehab. We have gone through a lot of hardships together. In just one two-week period, her mother was diagnosed with a brain bleed and we were told she'd be dead in the next couple of days. One of her two brothers was on the streets using again. The second brother, who'd been released from prison after 15 years, was re-arrested and headed back to prison. Then to top it all off, her daughter, my stepdaughter, was using and just found out that she was pregnant. In that two weeks, my wife and I still found time to laugh and make the most of the situation. We could've gone back out and started using again because of the pressure, but we didn't. We laughed about how that was not really an option. It would just make things worse.

If I was to say the number one thing my wife and I have together, it would be trust. Death was near when we first locked eyes. Darkness was in the depths of our souls. We first met when we were at our worst. We have always had a common bond, a common respect for one another. A lot of that stems from showing one another our vulnerabilities. Being honest, even when we thought it might disgust the other, helped strengthen the bond. That raw honesty was attractive to both of us. Because of that, trusting one another was never a concern. We both believe that trusting one another is what matters most.

When we disagree on something, we remain calm. Well, not always; we get irritated with one another at times. But because of that respect for one another, we never cross that line of disrespect. We've been through too much with addiction. So, when we get irritated with one another, one of us cracks a joke every single time. Nothing is serious enough to break our bond. When my wife and I have a problem, we confront it. That was imbedded in our heads in rehab—confront that shit immediately. When we get frustrated with one another, we're not allowed to leave the room until the matter is resolved. Usually when I get into an argument, I flee the scene ASAP. With her, I could no longer do that; we had to confront the issue and resolve it quickly. Because of that, we rarely have issues with one another. There are times I think I'm right, and she's wrong. She feels the opposite. No big deal. Because of the respect we have for one another we accept it as a difference of opinion. It's as if we need to make a business decision, versus an emotional decision. Even though these situations have everything to do with emotions, we try to find the resolution quickly. What is the most logical outcome for this situation? We try our best to find that every time we have a difference. It's not easy to do, but it helps.

After a few years of sobriety and practicing the theory of "every single moment of every single day" I slowly felt peace within my soul. I say slowly, because it takes time and consistency. I connected with my true self. It's like being under water. Everything sounds muffled. You can vaguely hear your surroundings, but you can't make out what that sound is. Once you finally surface, you know what the source of the noise is. The clarity of your true identity is present. All those years of your mind being drowned out by the chaos of drugs and/or alcohol, have now come to surface. With that resurfacing comes all your senses. You smell the oxygen in the air. You taste the purity of life on your tongue. You see the beauty in all your surroundings. More importantly, you feel the texture of love within your heart and soul.

I believe that loving your life, family and friends, and yourself are the three most important areas to focus on to live a life of happiness.

Life itself is an experience. Whether you see it as a good one or a bad one, that's up to you. When I say that you should love your life, I mean that you should love your physical surroundings, your mental and emotional states of mind, and your all-around day-to-day operations. Life after addiction provides a new opportunity for self-identity. In our addiction, we were lost, in our sobriety, we are presented with opportunity. When you choose to love your day-to-day life, then life itself becomes easier to deal with. When you feel love for your life, then you are far less likely to relapse.

Family and friends are those who stuck with you no matter what. Maybe they needed a break from you because of your addiction issues, but they always loved you and have been waiting for your return. I'm a strong believer in being a part of a group. I believe communication is medicine. When you're a part of a group, and play a role in it, you feel you have purpose. When that group consists of people you trust, a huge amount of stress is no longer a part of your daily life. Addiction pushes us away from those that we love the most. When you reach sobriety, then you're able to reconnect with loved ones and feel a sense of purpose again.

Self-love doesn't need to be an overwhelming feeling of self-confidence. When we get clean, we are very vulnerable and susceptible to self-esteem issues. Learning to love ourselves again takes time. It's like a very slow-moving snowball effect. But with practice, you can build upon that self-love. When you give someone a compliment, have you noticed that it feels good to do so? Deep down inside you know that means a lot to them. Do the same thing to yourself. Look in the mirror every single day and give yourself a compliment. You've got to say it like you mean it. You have to believe in it. You have to know that these words are going to make a difference. Say it with a smile on your face, and make sure that person in the mirror feels your sincerity, your passion, and your honesty.

Going through my addiction and the addition of withdrawals, I felt the full effects of life's gravity. That gravity led to rehab, which opened my eyes to a vast amount of knowledge pertaining to who I truly was. While searching for who I was, I had to experience adversity. I had to confront my demons. My perspective on life started to change for the better. I remembered stories like the one I've written in another chapter about the butterfly, and how that reminded me of my ability to achieve a goal. With that, every choice I make from here on out will determine if I can maintain sobriety. I want to make better choices versus bitter choices. I now want to keep my values at the forefront of my daily routine.

And above all else, I need to be passionate about my sobriety. I need to be passionate about life. I need to continue taking leaps of faith. While releasing all of that positive passion I need to keep things in balance. My greatest accomplishment with balance is the acceptance of both good and evil living within me. I accept that. In fact, I love that.

Love is what I yearned for since I was a child. I traveled down a road that I thought would never allow me to turn back. It turned out that my addiction didn't let me turn back, it took me straight home. My addiction got me home through the efforts I've made in my sobriety. Sobriety has been an eye-opening experience. My newfound love is 100 percent me. It just so happened that love turned out to be the greatest emotional experience I've ever had.

In the end, aren't we all chasing dopamine? We all want to feel happiness and we'll go to great lengths to feel that. Think of a list of words that describe happiness or positivity. Like joy, happiness, calm, euphoria, peace, honesty, commitment, sensation, good, grand, great, bliss, and the list goes on. In the end, when you combine any of those words, it is love that creates that feeling. When you are emotionally committed to someone or something, you feel love. When you feel peace within your body and soul, you feel love. When you experience feeling bliss, you feel love.

Drugs gave us a feeling of happiness, warmth, and peace. That's what made drugs so beautiful. Unfortunately, that comes at a cost, because drugs will in fact turn on you. I can either drink beer and feel the quick effects of euphoria, then pay the price of pain, or I can eat kale and be patient, and in time feel the effects of euphoria with no negative consequence. Sobriety has shown me that the dopamine that I so desperately searched for in my addiction was attainable in my sobriety with patience and hard work.

I have heard numerous times throughout my life that we only use 10 percent of our brain, leading us to think about the possibilities of the mind. I feel the same way about love. I believe our journey here on Earth will only allow us to feel 10 percent of love, no matter how intense your love is for others—family, friends, spouse, etc.—you will only experience love at a 10 percent capacity.

That makes me think in a broader way. I've always been intrigued by the reports of people who have died and been revived. The cliché is that they saw beauty, light, and felt overwhelming peace. Their descriptions lead me to think that life after death might be pure love.

No matter where you are, who you're with, when you arrive in the afterlife you feel 100 percent pure love. If my 10 percent theory is correct, then death sounds beautiful. Like anything else good, you've got to earn it. For me to obtain 100 percent in the afterlife I have to put forth the effort in this current one. Everything in life is earned whether it's this life or the next. That's my belief. I choose to believe that because it's exciting to think and feel that life after death is pleasant. This belief system allows me to focus on maximizing my 10 percent while I'm here. It also reminds me to give this sobriety thing everything I have. Go hard, be the best you, and get your 10 percent every day you're here. That's how you obtain 100 percent in the afterlife. Love life to the fullest while you are here, then one day this will all make sense.

Love life! Love your family and friends! Most of all, love yourself!

Dave Atherton is a dynamic speaker and lecturer. His message is one of optimism, humor, and inspiration. To have him speak to your group or organization contact him through Undeviating LLC: undeviatingpaths.com, or email him at dave@undeviatingpaths.com

About the Author

Dave Atherton is a recovering addict, writer and speaker. Currently, he is also working on videos depicting the art of addiction, withdrawal symptoms, and recovery. He currently works in the mental health field working directly with adult clients. Dave is married to his wife Brandie, is a father to his daughter Justice, and a grandfather to his grandson Justus-James. Dave currently lives in Reno, Nevada.